MW01118138

MAKE UNSTOPPABLE SIMPLE

MAKE
UNSTOPPABLE
SIMPLE

CREATIVE PROBLEM SOLVING IN LIFE AND LEADERSHIP

DINA B. SIMON

rockpaperstar

ISBNs: 978-0-9835887-3-3 (hardcover);
978-0-9835887-2-6 (paperback);
978-0-9835887-4-0 (ePub);
978-0-9835887-5-7 (Kindle)

Printed in the United States of America
First Printing: 2015

19 18 17 16 15   5 4 3 2 1

Cover and interior design by Ryan Scheife / Mayfly Design
Illustrations by Kim Siebold / Kim Siebold Studio's

RockPaperStar Press
333 Washington Ave. N Suite 300
Minneapolis, MN 55401

For large orders or speaking or consulting requests,
please contact (612) 470-STOP

CONTENTS

CHAPTER 4

CHAPTER 5

CHAPTER 6

CHAPTER 7

PREFACE

Unstoppable. A word that I have used to describe myself from time to time, and a word that has been used to describe the energy I bring to life or a situation. I have had life experiences that have stopped me in my tracks—sometimes for a minute, sometimes for months or years. Through reflection on my journey, I have found some key ways that have enabled me to move forward. I share these *Unstoppable* behaviors with you because I know there are others who will benefit from my story. Most people have had similar situations and similar stories to share, and my "call to action" for those who want to share their stories is to do so—I would love to know about them, and we can keep telling *Unstoppable* stories together. This book was written to take you through the story of my journey and teachings in hopes that it will inspire you to look at your own journey and your own *"Unstoppableness."*

I have many people in my life to thank, including my husband and daughter and entire extended family and my close inner circle network! As you read through my story you will learn about those who have been instrumental in allowing me to grow. I dedicate this book to my godmother and aunt, Margaret Joan Vigard White. She predicted I would write a book one day! Her love and support through all my years of life has fed my *Unstoppableness!*

A special thank you to Michelle LeBow of Memoir of Me! Michelle, when you walked into my life this book was on the shelf. Quickly we became Unstoppable together. Thank you for lending me your amazing talents!

I also dedicate this book to the three people who stepped up to push me forward: Jeff Brown, who continues to be my daily multiplier and motivation to activate on the things I set out to do! Without his coaching and encouragement, this book might not have been completed! Jeffrey Hayzlett, for his continued belief in me that I might have something to share with the world and who asks me to show up in life and continue my life's journey! My dear friend and publisher, Cathy Paper, who asked only one question: "What do you need?" We partnered to be *Unstoppable* together on getting this book to print. I look forward to RockPaperStar Press being tied to what we do for years to come!

Cheers and be *Unstoppable*!

INTRODUCTION

As I set out to write this book, a great friend of mine, Jeff Brown, whom you will hear more about in later chapters, sat down and helped me frame out messaging. We talked about my leadership journey and the road map of my life. I described the milestones and events and how I worked through them. When he asked the question, "How did it feel when you were going through those really hard times?" my response was, "It sucked." We talked about naming the book *Un-suck What Sucks*! We landed on *Make Unstoppable Simple* because we discovered there were some simple things I was able to put in place in my life that allowed me to be *Unstoppable*. As hard as times can be, there are some simple ways to navigate and find solutions to move you forward in times when you think moving forward is not an option.

Around the same time that Jeff and I were ideating, I was preparing for a workshop with a group of women that required me to map out my leadership journey, the highs and the lows of my life. This exercise allows you to look at what has happened in the past, where you are today, and where are you going in the future. Through this exercise a few things resonated over and over with me. I realized they were the simple things I do or activate when things are really hard! The story of *Make Unstoppable Simple* became pretty clear.

I have been told I have moxie (my Uncle Karl would say that about me when I was a very young girl before I knew what it even meant, but I loved that he thought I had it!). I am tenacious. I am asked if I plug myself in at night due to my energy level. I have been called a bitch. I have been called a trailblazer. I have been called lucky. I have been told I can be a bulldozer and I need to be careful not to knock people down in the wake of my path. These are the descriptors that bring me back to the word *Unstoppable*. I have the willpower to move mountains to do what needs to get done. Certainly, I have no intention of knocking someone down or hurting anyone in the process. The understanding of how others perceive me and how, as a leader, I must adjust to those around me has helped me grow in leadership maturity.

Take a journey with me as I share my story, and reflect on your own life and the challenges you have faced. Ask yourself along the way how your leadership journey has allowed you to grow into who you are today. How can you tap into those strengths to allow you to be *Unstoppable* in what you are trying to accomplish?

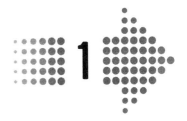

My Pinnacle Moment

The summer after I had left my role as a vice president managing $500 million in sales of a $2 billion organization to slow down and simplify my life, my daughter, Mandi, walked into the kitchen after dinner on an ordinary weeknight. I was scrubbing the countertop. She was about to turn eight and she had ideas. She said, "I want to start a company that helps kids."

"That's nice." I was half listening to her and I turned my back to Mandi to spray down the sauté pan in the sink. Mandi continued, "You know, helping the kids in North Minneapolis." I stopped the sink sprayer, turned around, and sat down at the table with her. I asked her to tell me more. She smiled at me with her retainer in her mouth. The summer's night breeze floated through the open window and splayed her bangs across her forehead. She said, "I want to start a company to raise money for the kids who don't have a home because of the tornado in Minneapolis."

I grabbed my iPad. I started to interview her to learn about what she had in her head. She explained her business plan, which involved starting a car wash to raise eight hundred dollars. I have to admit, I was impressed. Her business plan even included revenue projections for her first event.

Mandi's focus and passion for this project continued to grow for weeks. It was as if she felt responsible for taking action and doing something for these kids. We called around to people in our community to see if they would sponsor Mandi under their nonprofit umbrella for her to raise money for her cause. We were reminded that if she were to fundraise under someone's umbrella, the funds would go back to their organization and distributed to those they serve. Mandi was pretty passionate about creating something that she could design and determine how to distribute the funds. An accountant we talked to joked with me and said, "Dina, it sounds like you are starting your own nonprofit." The seed was planted.

Personally, I had written checks to nonprofits, but I certainly hadn't had even a minute to volunteer with a nonprofit nor be actively involved in one to know how to start or run one. I explained to her the difference between a for-profit company and a nonprofit, and that if she wanted to do what she was describing, it was the latter. In the next moments we started talking about what we could name her nonprofit. With the last name Simon, Mandi immediately started with the Simon Says game, and we both started throwing words out there. Then Mandi said, "Simon Says Give." I ran into the office and Mandi followed me. She watched over my shoulder as I frantically typed at the computer and locked down everything with that name. I knew there was something magical about to happen.

In a short period of time, we were moving fast-forward in building a full-fledged 501c3. It was as if everything in my life had led me to this singular *Unstoppable* moment in the kitchen with Mandi. I call this moment of clarity in Mandi's idea my *Pinnacle Moment*, and this moment is the reason I can share my leadership journey. My *Pinnacle Moment* happened mainly because I had simplified my life. When Mandi started talking, I was able to

. . . .

My *Pinnacle Moment* happened mainly because I had simplified my life.

. . . .

shut everything else out and listen. In this *Pinnacle Moment*, I had a gut feeling that this was more than my young daughter having an idea, and I took a leap of faith with the support of those telling us to go for it. We were able to run fast—we were able to be clear in what it was we needed help with and people lined up to help in the areas in which they could. We needed a lot of help! We were starting from the ground up. What in the world did I know about starting a nonprofit?

As we started to build this nonprofit, we started with our relationships within our community. The first check we received was from a former client, and I knew if I accepted her check, I would be forced to move things forward and become a legitimate organization—another defining moment where everything happens for a reason. If Jacque hadn't written a check to me that day, we might not have ever really moved forward. Almost at the same time Jacque Fiegel wrote the check, Jeff Brown entered my life. Jeff was immediately supportive of Mandi's idea and vision. We continued to move fast forward. Our 501c3 application was approved within ninety days.

Coming from a corporate background and having the opportunity to sit around some large boardroom tables in my career, I knew that the best way to assemble a board of directors for any organization, for-profit or nonprofit, is with the key areas covered.

I set out to build that team. We have all aspects covered: an attorney, a CPA, an educator, a marketing guru, a strategic business coach, an executive coach, human resources, etc. Our organizational chart is an impressive one. Several of the team members have their doctorates and several have spent so much time in their field that they have honorary ones. When people take a look at who lined up early on to support us, the immediate response has always been, "Wow, you have an amazing board of directors." The credibility of our team immediately showed we meant business—this wasn't just a fleeting idea from a seven-year-old girl. These accomplished professionals weren't going to tie their names and reputations to something they didn't believe.

Our committee and volunteer teams quickly raised their hands to support and help us. Companies and clients I had worked with in the past continued to line up to support us! Our corporate sponsors have been extraordinary and a testimony to the value of relationships. Jim Johnson is a franchisee of the staffing firm I was at and he approached me after we launched to ask how he could support Mandi. What grew from that conversation at a Caribou Coffee is the branding of High Five for Supplies™.

High Five for Supplies is a backpack and supplies drive we do each summer in honor of Mandi's August birthday. Since she was five years old, she has asked for donations for her birthday. With an August birthday, she thought about providing kids with what they needed to go back to school. Once Simon Says Give was in place, Jim helped formalize the drive and the branding. We consider him Mandi's co-founder of the High Five for Supplies drive, and he will forever be tied to our story.

Jim and his team continue to be our partners in the drive in Minneapolis and St. Paul with hundreds of Jim's clients engaging in the mission. Jim is a prime example of *Unstoppable* relationships. We were thrown together in a professional situation—he was one of my top franchisees in the company (he still is, I am just no longer at the company) and even almost four years after I left the organization, I probably talk to him more than I did when we worked together. We collaborate on many things and he has been an amazing partner and inspiration to pushing our Simon Says Give agenda forward. Simon Says Give was on our *Unstoppable* journey!

From that moment in the kitchen with Mandi, Simon Says Give and Simon Says Lead have continued to build. A few months later, I attended a happy hour event for a company where I helped launch their human resources staffing practice, and one of the owners grabbed my arm and asked me to come meet someone. He introduced me to the new CIO of the Deluxe Corporation, Mike Mathews. Mike immediately connected me to Julie Loosbrock, a senior vice president of Deluxe, because he thought Julie needed to hear our story.

The connection with Julie has been instrumental in moving Simon Says Give forward. Julie has adopted Mandi and her mission and has put herself and her organization behind us, helping us succeed. Deluxe donated one hundred birthdays in a box in 2013, and in 2014 they sponsored our design contest where kids across the country could submit designs for the notebook covers that went into our backpacks. Julie enlisted her partner in crime, Pete, who made it happen. It's been an amazing partnership.

Chris Ohlendorf and Tony Sorensen are the two owners of the staffing firm that introduced me to Deluxe and are another classic example of *Unstoppable* relationships. Whenever I have needed anything over the past few years, they have shown up. When we needed forty volunteers to work a phone bank for the High Five for Supplies drive that our CBS station was going to do for us, they filled fifteen of those spots. When we needed hundreds of volunteers to help us with the packing and sorting of backpacks, they sent over forty volunteers two years in a row to help.

From my *Pinnacle Moment* of clarity—simplifying and shutting out the clutter of life and listening to my daughter instead of

. . . .

Through my story, I hope to share how you can gain this clarity to begin your own *Unstoppable* journey.

. . . .

finishing the dishes—we have now built a viable, growing non-profit agency. This singular *Unstoppable* moment is what brings me to share my life and leadership story. Through my story, I hope to share how you can gain this clarity to begin your own *Unstoppable* journey.

How to Make Unstoppable Simple

In my leadership and life journey, building up to my recent moment of clarity to help start Simon Says Give and Simon Says Lead, I've developed a model to gain clarity of purpose to move along an *Unstoppable* journey. In the un-STOP-able model, we have pulled out the acronym STOP. The STOP model will show you how to tap into your *Pinnacle Moments* of clarity in your life.

Four Simple Steps to Unstoppable

1. **Simplify** | Simplify to scrutinize and spot the challenges you want to solve.
2. **Talents** | Identify the unique talents you bring to the table.
3. **Others** | Build relationships with the people who can help you.
4. **Plan** | Build a solid plan that will actively move you toward your goal.

6

LET'S PUT THE MODEL TO THE TEST!

SIMPLIFY
to scrutinize and
spot the challenge
you want to solve

The S Is for Simplify in the STOP Model

First, let's take a look at the S in the STOP model. The S is to Simplify. The first step to finding clarity in purpose to lead you on your *Unstoppable* journey is around simplifying to scrutinize and spot the real and true challenges in your life and leadership. Simplifying to remove the clutter that may prevent you from listening when you have a moment like I did in the kitchen with Mandi. If I hadn't slowed down and simplified my life—where I blocked out all the noise—I may have missed my moment. The moment that has led us to the *Unstoppable* journey.

There are several moments in my life where I've simplified to solve challenges. This collection of moments has led me to finding the clarity to move and act to bring Simon Says Give and Simon Says Lead to life.

My Mom's Death

When I was twelve, the image of my pretty normal family fell apart when my mom committed suicide. Today, thirty-some years later, the word suicide is a bit more mainstream and not something that is said in a whisper. Thirty-some years ago, it was as if suicide was the plague, something that wasn't spoken about and something that quickly defined not just my mom's life, but those of us left behind.

My mom had filed for divorce from Dad (they hadn't been happy for years) and she was scared to death to be responsible for her daughters. My older sister, Debbie, was now off at her first year of college; my little sister and I would continue to live in our childhood home with Mom. Mom suffered from depression and had a drinking problem—two things I didn't know much about as a child or see with my young eyes. This was the first death I had experienced as a child, and I felt so confused and alone without my mom or the support of being emotionally close to my dad.

Every moment of those days and weeks leading up to her death and the days and weeks after she was gone are so vivid—it's as if it happened yesterday. I didn't know what the word "suicide" meant. I remember my Uncle Karl asking in a hushed voice if there was a note and the horrified look on his face. My dad and my grandma didn't want to explain what suicide meant to protect me, and yet there was no way to hide what had happened.

I remember the drama about who would be invited to the funeral. I was twelve and I remember every moment of hurt, confusion, and embarrassment. Even in these painful moments, I remember shutting out much of the noise by excusing myself to my room. My grandma didn't want to invite non-family members or even extremely close friends to the funeral—I believe she thought if people didn't attend the funeral, it would cause less embarrassment to our family. One person in particular whom my grandma didn't want to invite was Mom's good friend and former neighbor, Dorothy. Dorothy and my aunt had found my mom after her death and my aunt thought we should invite Dorothy to the funeral.

I remember taking myself out of the heated discussion between my aunt and my grandma and going to my room. In the

. . . .

I quickly learned about suicide and what it meant to be a kid whose mom decided to take her own life.

. . . .

quiet respite, on my green and yellow bedspread—the very bedspread my mom had tucked me into a few nights before—I simplified to solve the challenge. Dorothy knew my mom killed herself and preventing her from attending the funeral wouldn't change that fact. I also was certain my mom would want Dorothy at the funeral. At that moment, I knew I would make sure she would be invited to the funeral. I walked back to the kitchen and told my grandma, "If Dorothy doesn't come to the funeral, then I won't go either."

I'll never forget the look on my grandma's face. This was the moment where I learned when I simplified to solve, I would find the clarity to act. This is one of the first times that I used this strategy to move forward and act in an authentic way. To this day, I am still using the S in STOP to move forward and act.

I quickly learned about suicide and what it meant to be a kid whose mom decided to take her own life. I remember very vividly those amazing cousins, aunts, and uncles who showed up, really showed up in my life from the age of twelve and beyond. I watched my Grandma Benny (my mom's mom) go through her own journey of losing a child, and watched her take care of her granddaughters at the same time. Both Grandma Benny and my aunts stepped into the role of surrogate moms for us. I can't imagine what I would have done without her throughout my life, especially those first years after losing my mom.

Chicken Pox

My mom was my world. I don't just say that because she's gone. We truly were close. There's not a childhood memory that doesn't include my mom as part of the story. One of my favorite memories of my mom is when she would say to me, "Have I hugged my kid today?" She'd hold me so close, wrapping me bear-hugged in her arms and folding me into her body next to her soft skin. She was my rock, my safety net, and my sunshine. My mom treated me as her little angel who could do no wrong. My nickname was (and still is with family and childhood friends) "Beans" because I was always full of trouble as a kid—but she always just saw me as her girl.

When I was in the third grade I had a terrible case of the chicken pox. Every inch of my body was covered in red pox, even my eyelids. I found a way to milk my illness, and I missed an entire six weeks of school. It really came down to the fact that I wanted to be home with my mom! My mom made me bacon and eggs every morning, and in the afternoons we watched *All My Children* and *General Hospital* together. Then, I would help her cook supper or help her make the beds and clean the bathroom sinks. I believe I knew these one-on-one moments with my mom would be some of my most treasured memories.

My sister Debbie would tell you that my favorite teacher in elementary school was the nurse, Mrs. Brown, because she saw me more than any teacher I had for class. After I recovered from the chicken pox, I learned that if I told them I had a stomachache they couldn't tell if I was truly faking it. The more I went to the nurse to complain meant the more I got to be home with my mom. I used the S in STOP—slowing down and simplifying to listen in the *Unstoppable* journey—even when I had chicken pox or when I took a timeout on Mrs. Brown's cot. These moments of slowing down, even if I didn't realize it at the time, have become some of the most important moments in my life journey.

. . . .

These moments of slowing down, even if I
didn't realize it at the time, have become
some of the most important moments
in my life journey.

. . . .

My Therapist

After about a year of being on autopilot and not necessarily
dealing with the entire situation at hand, I hit my head during
a snow tubing accident in the seventh grade. I was diagnosed
with a concussion—it was the first time I had been sick since my
mom's death and I wanted only my mommy to take care of me. I
mourned my mom's death after my head injury and I felt the very
opposite of *Unstoppable* during the next year.

My aunt made sure my dad sent me to a therapist. The first
time I sat in my therapist's office, squinting my eyes at the sun-
light that flickered through the leaded windows and tapping my
foot on the knotted oak floors, I wanted to run down the hallway
and out of that old building. Her name was Dr. Killkelly. I will
never forget her name or her dark hair that reminded me of my
mom. I saw her two times a week for months as I worked through
the head injury and dealt with the loss of my mom. The hours
of hard work I put in with Dr. Killkelly helped me put the pieces
back together so I could feel *Unstoppable* again.

One afternoon, I sat slumped in Dr. Killkelly's big blue chair
and thought, "I don't care what she says, I can just kill myself if I
want to." The question ran through my mind over and over, "My
mom did it, why can't I?" I loved her so much and she took her
life. Should I?

In these moments sitting across from Dr. Killkelly, I stopped and simplified. Sometimes I didn't talk to her the whole hour. Sometimes she would sit there with me without talking, and other times she would talk about what she was going to cook for supper to fill the space. Sometimes I would talk the whole hour without letting her get a word in edgewise. Either way, these were the quiet and simple moments to reflect and scrutinize my life. Twice a week for fifty-two weeks, I met with Dr. Killkelly. It was in these moments in her office where I began to find clarity in my purpose after my mom's death. I understood that I would take responsibility for my family and take care of—at first in my adolescent way, and then into my early adulthood—my younger sister. I also knew I had to make some changes. I needed a new place to continue in the next phase of my life's journey. In Dr. Killkelly's office, I gained the clarity I needed to face my future.

Totino-Grace

Shortly after the year in Dr. Killkelly's office, I was in eighth grade. I walked upstairs into the kitchen where my dad was making a peanut butter and jelly sandwich for my little sister's lunch. I said, "Dad, I want to go to Totino-Grace next year." He spread the peanut butter over the bread. I lifted my head and continued to explain that I had found Totino-Grace—a Catholic high school about twenty minutes away—and this was the place I needed to go for the next four years of my life. There must have been something in my voice or in the way I had walked into the room, because he put the bread down on the countertop and listened to me that day.

Dad and I toured the school together. I think he liked that it was a Catholic school and I think he understood I needed a fresh, new experience, where kids weren't looking at me as the girl who had a mom who killed herself. Totino-Grace is another example of simplifying to solve the challenge. Thankfully, I had the support of my dad to allow me to move and act with clarity on the next phase of my *Unstoppable* journey.

Adoption

When you really take the time to reflect back on your life, starting from how you came into this world, you discover so many points in time that define and continue to define who you are today.

I was placed up for adoption as a baby. I went to foster care for six weeks before my parents got me on St. Patrick's Day. I celebrate my birthday and my "gotcha day." I reflect often on the decision that my birth mom made in delivering me and placing me for adoption. She could have made a different decision and I would not be physically here today. If she made the decision to keep me and raise me, my life and my journey would not be what it is today.

My adopted mom and dad had married and started a family with my older sister. After several years of trying to get pregnant again without success, my parents adopted me. Being adopted was always something I loved about myself—there was never anything I found negative about it. After my adoption, my mom did get pregnant again with my little sister. Our family became a family of three girls and I would use my adoption to my advantage. I would say to my sisters, "I am so glad I am adopted." Being adopted made me feel special, like I had a special gift that was all my own and I was different from my sisters. I remember only one time when my little sister was mad at me and she asked my mom, "Why did we have to adopt her anyway?" I'm sure it was a normal feeling she had at times, but she only voiced this feeling once, in anger.

· ·

My life's journey of being adopted has moved full-circle from me being an adopted daughter to being an adoptive mom.

· ·

Anyone who knew our family would never suspect that I was adopted—I have amazingly similar features to all of my sisters and my mom and dad. Even to this day, a woman at a party said to me, "You must be Deb's sister. You look just like her." I love that I am adopted and I blend into my family—both physically and emotionally—in a way that makes us a perfect fit.

My life's journey of being adopted has moved full-circle from me being an adopted daughter to being an adoptive mom. After being married to my husband, Rich, for several years and having a high-powered career, I wanted to be a mom more than anything else. I especially wanted to be a mom to a little girl. I wanted to have a daughter with whom I could do all the things that my mom and I didn't have the opportunity to do.

We had been married for about seven years and not yet able to have children. Many of my friends have faced similar situations and have chosen different paths to have a family. Many of my girlfriends wanted to experience childbirth; they felt they needed to try everything they could in order to have that experience. I had no problem with not going through childbirth—I have never felt the need to experience childbirth myself. My own personal experiences of adoption have led me to be perfectly comfortable with adopting a baby of our own.

The adoption process today is a bit different than the one my parents went through. My adoption was closed, and that's why I went to foster care for six weeks until the paperwork went through and I could safely be placed with my parents. Today, "open adoption" is the term. When we met our adoption attorney—one of the best in the country who wrote much of the law for open adoptions in the United States—she shared with us the openness of an adoption these days. An open adoption?

This was another S moment where I had to simplify to gain clarity before I could move forward. I had been expecting the same situation my parents had when I was adopted. Open adoption means we could have a relationship with the birth parents— that type of relationship seemed bizarre to me at the time. Many choose foreign adoptions for that reason—they don't want to have a relationship or connection in any way.

Once I started scrutinizing what the true challenge for me was in this situation, I realized what is most important to me is that there are so many children here in the United States who need a home. Additionally, I have my own life experience of being adopted into a loving family. After I simplified the problem, I made the decision that an open adoption process was the right choice for us.

I found my *Unstoppableness* in the processes. We signed paperwork with our attorney in April 2003, and immediately we got phone calls with situations for children who may have some difficulties and challenges due to conception. For example, if a baby was conceived due to rape or if the baby might have issues with drugs from the birth mother, we could say no. Morally and ethically, I had a difficult time with this idea—when you get pregnant you get what you get, so is it moral or ethical for us to be selective with an adopted baby?

I remember pulling my car off the road to have conversations with our adoption attorney about some of these children. I listened in these moments; she helped coach us through the pros and cons and provided expert advice so we could make informed decisions. We did say no to a lot of situations before we said yes.

Finally, an opportunity arose for us and we flew to Oklahoma City from San Francisco to meet with and be interviewed by a birth mother as she was getting ready to have her baby. We spent time with her and it seemed that this baby would be ours.

After a few weeks back home, we got a call stating that the birth mom had had the baby and if we could get to the hospital by midnight to take custody of the child, the child was ours. Again, we lived in San Francisco, and the baby was born in Oklahoma City—not an easy trek, and certainly not an easy one with minutes of notice. We made it in time to Oklahoma, and we literally ran into the hospital at about 11:30 p.m.—but we made it! We took that baby girl home to an apartment that the adoption social workers on that end had arranged for us.

The waiting period before we could legally leave the state was about two weeks. Both Rich and I had to take leaves from our jobs and round up our friends to house-sit our dogs. And yet, as I sat in the rented apartment living room in Oklahoma City, we had a beautiful baby girl in our arms and I cried in relief. My in-laws live in Dallas and drove up to be with us; they were excited to welcome their new granddaughter into the family.

Three days into feeding her bottles and changing her diapers and waking up with her in the middle of the night, the birth mom changed her mind about the baby. She and her family decided to keep the baby. She was within her legal rights to do so, and she took the baby from us. There is nothing to explain the heartbreak I felt. The one thing I had been so afraid of, "What if the birth mom changes her mind and takes the baby?" had happened to us.

After going through this heartbreak, I wasn't sure I could ever go through it again with another baby. I told our attorney I needed a year before we talked. I was stopped—I was no longer *Unstoppable.* I needed time to simplify, to find a way to deal with

CHAPTER 2

Sometimes you don't get to choose the next moment when life's journey is going to change.

this loss. For me, it was more than the loss of that child being ours. For me, it was the loss of all that time and emotion and investment—and walking away with nothing. The energy it was going to take to face all the people who worried about this situation happening in the first place.

Sometimes you don't get to choose the next moment when life's journey is going to change. My life's moment came only a few short weeks later when our attorney called. She chose to share this "perfect" situation with my husband, Rich, first.

Rich called me while I was driving home from a meeting about two hours away. His words came in choppy sentences through the phone. The baby had been born. The baby is in a nearby city. The birth mom herself is adopted. The birth mom is young and healthy. I hung the phone up on him.

I pulled the car into a gas station, turned the engine off, and rested my forehead on the steering wheel. I pounded on the dashboard. I wanted a year. A year to heal. It had only been a few weeks! I called Rich back—I think I probably hung up on him a few times in that gas station parking lot—and yet I felt myself start to move, a chipping away, a small spot in my heart at first, and then bigger.

I put the car back in drive. I'm not sure if the car was on autopilot that evening, because I don't remember seeing one stoplight or road sign on that drive home. However, by the time I pulled into the garage two hours later, I had made up my mind. In all my life, up to this point, when I have experienced loss, I experience rich joy on the other end. This child might be my next moment in my life's journey. Even in my fearfulness, I knew Rich and I had to move forward in the process with this baby.

We went and met the birth parents for our "interview." We were one of three couples. I was still afraid. And yet, we had a few good things about this adoption scenario that pushed me forward. The baby was in the same state as we were and California didn't have a twelve-day waiting period—if the birth parents signed away their parental rights, she would be ours.

We met with the baby's birth parents on Saturday. Rich and I went home to wait. The very next day, we got the call. "We want you to be her parents." The words rolled over and over in my head until the next evening when we picked her up at her birth mother's house.

I'll never forget the moment Mandi—a beautiful baby girl—was placed in my arms. That one moment has led me to the amazing journey that is my life. Even more, I have been taken aback by how fulfilling our lives have become with the increased level of intimacy we've experienced in our blended family structure with Mandi's birth parents. We started in a place of anxiety and awkwardness—the open adoption process was new for all of us—and yet, fairly quickly, we have become truly an extended family moving through our lives together.

Mandi has made me a mother and before I became her mom, I didn't understand when our attorney told us, "You will come to learn that you can never have too many people who love your child." In my naïveté as a new mom, I couldn't be prepared to share my daughter with anyone quite yet. I now fully claim to understand that Mandi really can't have too many people love her. Our multi-faceted family members who love her have shaped the fabric of who she is and how she approaches her life and her

I'll never forget the moment Mandi—a beautiful baby girl—was placed in my arms.

relationships. The photos of her with her birth parents all over her room and photos of her with us make up Mandi's rich story. Lucky me, I'm the first person she sees in the morning, and I'm the one who snuggles with her before she gets up and ready for school in the morning.

Moving Back to Minnesota

We had been living in San Francisco away from our core family—my sisters, my aunts and uncles—for many years. When we became a family with Mandi, again I had a moment of clarity that led me to where we are now with Simon Says Give and Simon Says Lead.

I had stuck my two-year-old Mandi, still pajama-clad, in her car seat at six a.m. Rich was leaving for work thirty miles away and was dropping Mandi at her daycare. I threw my suitcase in my car trunk for my three-day work trip, as I did every week. I started my car next to Rich's car in the garage and I saw a sleepy-eyed Mandi wave at me through the car window as Rich pulled out of the driveway. That morning, something cracked in me. I wasn't sure I wanted to live this way anymore.

The next week, Mandi got sick while I was on the road. We couldn't take her to daycare because she had a fever and Rich had a meeting he couldn't reschedule at work. We didn't have any family to help us out in this moment. I sat in my field office, five hours away from Mandi when she wasn't feeling well, and I made up my mind.

That night, Rich and I made a plan to move from San Francisco back to the Midwest. We are both from the Midwest and ultimately we wanted to be closer to family. We set out to live in Minnesota, Illinois, or Wisconsin. We had to move where Rich could find a job in his field. He has a smaller niche of specialized work as a chemist and I could work in staffing from anywhere in the Midwest. Minnesota is where we landed and it worked perfectly to be close to my family. We wanted Mandi to grow up with aunts and uncles and cousins. We wanted a simpler lifestyle where we wouldn't have to get Mandi up at six a.m. to go to daycare.

The move simplified our life. We took time to settle in and discover what life we could make for ourselves while replanting some roots. I have become engaged in the community; the Twin Cities area is a huge network of people, and I've walked into as many places as possible to reconnect with old friends and meet new ones. The tapestry of this metro area is rich with accomplished people who are grounded in hard-working Midwestern values. The move back to Minnesota is another instrumental moment in our journey that has helped us build and grow Simon Says Give and Simon Says Lead.

Summary of the First Step in STOP Is S as in Simplify to Solve

The first step in being Unstoppable in our STOP model is to simplify, which enables you to scrutinize and spot the challenges you want to solve. Reflect on different moments in your life. How did you simplify to block out the noise and find the clarity to solve your challenge? Are there times when you didn't simplify and perhaps missed a Pinnacle Moment? How can you implement what it means for you to simplify to solve and find clarity in your life moments?

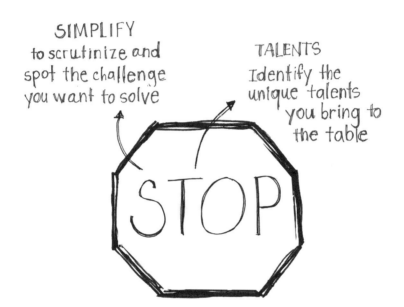

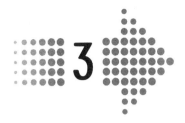

3

The T Is for Talents in the STOP Model

The second step in the STOP model is T. The T in STOP stands for talents. Once you've simplified to understand what you want to solve, the next step is to look inside to see what talents you have to help you solve this problem or challenge. The power of this exercise is to evaluate what you bring to the table—the innate talents you have and how these talents will move you to the next space. Talents are a critical component in the STOP model.

In the process of setting up our nonprofit, I evaluated what talents I brought to the table. I had never started my own business from the ground up, let alone a nonprofit. After my assessment, I determined my three top talents include relationship building, risk-taking, and work ethic/personal accountability. Relationship building: building and recruiting a team of people around us who had the expertise we needed. Risk-taking: making the leap and telling the story to gain interest in what we were doing. Work ethic and taking personal accountability: rolling up my sleeves to

. . . .

In the process of setting up our nonprofit, I evaluated what talents I brought to the table.

. . . .

do what it takes to move from start-up to thriving in the matter of a few short months. These three talents are what have led me to where I am now in building and growing Simon Says Give and Simon Says Lead.

Relationship Building

I learned early—in high school, building relationships with my teachers at Totino-Grace—about the importance of the people with whom you choose to surround yourself. I was missing a key relationship in my life: my mom. I understood at a young age that I had to build and create relationships with people who may not be part of my family to help me on my journey.

When I started at Totino-Grace, I aligned myself with two teachers in my freshman year. One was Sue Orlowski—the campus minister—and the other was Dick Paul, my math teacher and the vice principal. Together, we started "the greeting crew." Dick and I would stand in the hallway to say, "Hello!" to students in the morning. Seeing how our actions impacted each tired student who walked through the doors, Dick helped me find my leadership style in the locker-lined hallways of Totino-Grace. In the same vein, Sue helped me write a paper about the death of my mom during my freshman year. This paper expressed my innermost feelings about her death and was helpful in letting go and moving forward. My meaningful relationships with my two teachers guided me through my high school years and have extended into my adult life. This is the start of my understanding of how building and nurturing key relationships impacts the trajectory of my life.

As a leader, I believe you do not have to have all the answers, you have to have great people around you who can help find the answers. My talent in relationship building is one of my keys to

. . . .

As a leader, I believe you do not
have to have all the answers.

. . . .

success in leadership, and especially in building a team of people around me who are very different from me. I surround myself with people who complement my weaknesses and vice versa. Together, we make a great team. Together, we have the ability to divide and conquer to achieve greatness.

So often people are afraid to hire others who appear to be smarter or more successful. They feel they will lose power or control. What they gain is an inability to grow. How do you grow personally and professionally with clones or mediocrity around you? How does your business grow? Understanding your strengths and weaknesses and hiring around them will provide so many benefits.

The thing I've learned is that you don't have to be friends with those you work with. You have to get along and respect each other. What you share in common with the people you work with are an interest in the values of the organization you are serving and trusting in each other. As a leader you have to be willing to deal with difficult people and/or situations.

One of the relationship skills I am known for is working with people whom others have not wanted to work with. I find "difficult" people or situations a big challenge—bring it on! Have you ever worked for or with someone who was afraid to face what could be conflict or a negative situation? What happens? Everyone gets frustrated with the situation and the leader! Step up and walk through it.

I once had a team member who worked for me and people would roll their eyes when he would talk. They thought he was out in left field with his ideas and they didn't give him credit where credit was due. It drove me crazy. He wasn't trying to be difficult; he had something to share and contribute. Once we did a group exercise to talk about our team dynamics, people began to see he wasn't trying to be difficult. He really had something to share, he just was a huge outside-the-box thinker on a team full of in-the-box thinkers. He had to learn when to share what he wanted to share. He had to learn how to share his ideas while presenting his message. He learned it wasn't about being heard, it was about presenting to be understood. As a leader, the value of watching the relationship interactions and the change in dynamics was amazing.

The reward of stepping up as a leader to facilitate and change the perception of an individual who hadn't been taken seriously in the past was life changing for him and for me. He was able to see how a few changes in his style impacted his relationships with the team, and I was able to see how my influence as a leader impacted the team.

VICE PRESIDENT AT THIRTY-FIVE

At age thirty-five, I thought I had arrived. I had set goals and plans to be a vice president by then, and I had accomplished that. I was a vice president of a $2 billion company and was sitting at the leadership table with extremely talented and established people within my field. This organization is a franchised-based company, so the entrepreneurial spirit is even stronger than the company where I started my staffing career. I was in the field working to support my team of developers who supported the franchisees. This role was where I learned the most about leadership—what to do, what not to do, how to grow as a leader, and how to grow your capacity beyond what you thought possible.

As a young thirty-five-year-old female vice president, I was put to the test—especially in that first year. At one of the first regional meetings I attended, I was tasked with getting to know forty people in a room—about half of whom were franchisees and the other half key management in their offices. I was bombarded with questions about decisions that were being made back at headquarters. Good thing I can think on my feet, and good thing I was that middle kid who could throw herself in the middle of the room and say, "Hey, remember me?"

I guess I did a fine job because I heard a particular franchisee who had given me a lot of grief on his cell phone saying that he had drilled and grilled me and he thought I might be alright! That franchisee is a dear friend of mine all these years later—I respect his ability to say it like it is. I would rather have you give me the chance to be drilled or grilled—even in front of forty people—than talk behind my back. Bring it on.

My region was made up of eight developer regions, and all of them were or had been owners in the system with the organization since the early days—in other words, a ton of deep-rooted people. Most of the team was ten or more years older than me and many of them male. The role I stepped into was a newly created role for the company, and I was taking away a role some of the senior developers had previously played. The change in the organization caused some chaos. I showed up on the scene to lead and inspire a group of people who weren't really sure they wanted to work with me.

At this point, I knew it would take skillful relationship navigation to make it through this first year. I intellectually knew I could manage these relationships, and still there were times as soon as I was alone—I made sure this group never saw me—I would break down and cry. I remember a cousin of mine, someone extraordinarily successful in business and someone I love and respect a great deal, asked me, "Dina, why are you putting yourself through this? The deck is stacked too high!"

And yet, I saw this leadership challenge as a huge opportunity to work through and come out successful on the other end. I reflected so often on my journey of losing my mom during my first year as a vice president. Without knowing it at the time, this is one of the first moments I started defining and using the STOP model in this leadership opportunity. How did I need to simplify the problem? Who did I need to have in my life to help me through? What was my plan?

In the beginning of my role, there was one person—my boss—who really pushed me along. He might not have done it in the spirit of being a dynamic leader for me, but what he did with me was dynamic! He threw me into the ring and he was there when I needed him. He may have thought I was going to sink, but what he didn't know about me is that I'm a great swimmer! I was going to give it everything I had to be successful and *Unstoppable*. His leadership style was a perfect fit for my style. He coached me from the sidelines and allowed me to be autonomous and use my own authentic leadership style.

There were two people on my team who gave me the most heartache when I first started in this role. These two have become two of the most important relationships in my life to this day. The significance is in the power to work through even the toughest of relationships to see what might be on the other side. I had to use my relationship skills in ways I never had before to build these two relationships. Could I do it?

Keven Sasser and I were partnered in this new leadership role the first two years. I was a corporate vice president and he was a senior developer and long-time franchisee in the system on a contract with headquarters. We were to co-lead and inspire the team. We are very different people—he's analytical, and I'm intuitive and energetic.

With my knowledge of building strong relationships, I soon realized that I had to earn Keven's trust. With me, I trust immediately and let the relationship prove itself. Keven pushed me harder to see different points of view and challenge the lens I was seeing things through. I nagged and pushed him to see my point of view, and as he would say, I would wear him down with my energy and requests. As years went by, we built an amazing foundation! We can debate and agree to disagree and walk away without feeling beat-up—we value and respect our different perspectives.

It took a few years for Keven and me to get to that point. Years most people wouldn't have put the time into fighting through. And those who know both of us know Keven and I fought. After those years of working through the hard relationship dynamics, we developed an amazing *Unstoppable* relationship! If there is a life challenge I am facing and need a different perspective on it, whom do you think I call?

Having common values is the most important thing in building and sustaining relationships. The results of our relationship could have been very different—Keven and I could have decided to stay in different corners (sometimes we were pitted against each other); however, we have most of the very same values. These values hold us together even through our differences. When I call Keven, I call because I want his perspective. He is honest with me and his insight is important in my decision-making. He will challenge my thinking and my point of view. I don't enjoy criticism (who does?) and still, I value his feedback because I know it is most likely accurate.

Another key relationship in my growth that has led me to where I am today with Simon Says Give and Simon Says Lead is with my colleague and friend, Mark Tasler. Mark had also been on my team as a developer, was a senior leader within the franchise organization, and had been a part of the organization before it was formed. Mark also likes to push people to think and see things from different angles and different sides. He approaches things from "Big Thinking" and "Creative Ideas." Mark is curious and seeks out new ways to lead and inspire people. Mark and his wife, Sheryl, have created a successful business and legacy providing opportunities for thousands of employees over the years.

Mark is the one on my team who was geographically closest to me. Mark would pound his fists on the table fighting for his franchisees, and at first, I wasn't sure how to handle his behavior. And yet, as I grew closer to him, I knew he was truly fighting to support those around him—he wasn't fighting against me. We were able to quickly partner on some amazing work together. To this day, Mark and Sheryl have been our largest donors and supporters of Simon Says Give. They unconditionally support our efforts because of our relationship.

I could have stopped in my tracks in those early days when Mark would be pushing me to see his point of view. However, I engaged, I listened, and we agreed when we could agree. We agreed to disagree, and we walked away with ultimate respect for each other. My life is so much richer because I have him in my life. I would have missed out on so much if I had let those early interactions interfere with our relationship.

Mark is still someone whom I can count on to challenge me. I met him recently at an event, and he asked me about my five-year plan. He challenges me while offering his unwavering support and honesty. These are conversations I expect in my relationship with Mark. Similar to my experience with Keven in these situations, I want honest, meaningful feedback. In both of these key relationships in my life, I know I will be told the truth and pushed to see things differently. These two relationships have elevated me to where I am today with Simon Says Give and Simon Says Lead.

Risk-Taking

I moved out of my dad's house the minute I graduated from high school. I took the leap and left home and chose to attend the University of Minnesota my freshman year. I chose this college to be close to my younger sister who was just starting high school—my older sister also went there to be closer to us after Mom had died. I guess the three of us—sisters—really have watched out for each other all these years. These are the earliest moments I can remember of my T of risk-taking.

During my freshman year of college, I visited my best friend, Lisa, at the University of Wisconsin–Madison. I fell in love with Madison, and I made another risk-taking move to join Lisa my sophomore year. I took the risk to start a new life; however, this time I wasn't just starting at a new school, I was also starting out in a new town! I worked multiple jobs throughout college; I was a waitress at Chili's when a regular customer recruited me to work at a Madison-based company. A few years into my career with this company, they relocated to their headquarters in Dallas, Texas.

Again, I chose a risky move—I leapt from where I'd lived my whole life in the Midwest to the southern part of the United States. This had been my biggest leap of faith up to this point in my life, leaving my family behind. It was here, with this organization, that I found my launch pad to my professional career. I worked with a leadership team that was strictly male, and in Texas that means the old boys club. The team immediately saw my dedication and work ethic, and I was often recognized for my tenacity. This risk is where I learned the power of a strong leader:

the ability to walk into an office and be candid about what's going on or why something isn't working and offer solutions.

I reported to the president and vice president of the company, and I was just turning twenty-one. Pat Staudt, the vice president, was like a big brother. John Simon, the president, was like a father, and soon he actually became my father-in-law. Both of these men, and the other senior leadership team, taught me how to lead up, how to show up and navigate at a senior leadership table in those early years. They valued what I had to say and wanted my input. Their belief in me, even at this early stage in my career, was instrumental in my growth and in my career track.

The risk to move to Texas taught me one of my life's biggest lessons. The lesson, for me, is that through great risk comes great reward. The biggest reward of taking this risk to start a new life in Dallas was reuniting with my college friend Rich. John Simon, whom I worked for at this point, was Rich's dad. Rich relocated to Dallas for a summer internship soon after I had left Madison. He came into the office and I invited him to a volleyball game and happy hour. We've been together ever since that night! We married not long after he arrived in Dallas. Together, we took one more risk and moved to Tucson, Arizona, where he had been accepted into graduate school for his Ph.D. in analytical chemistry.

Most people probably wouldn't want to start over in another city (my third in four years). For me, I looked at this risk-taking as an opportunity to learn to engage with the culture and customs of new people. This new start in Arizona is where I took my next leap into what would become my career in the staffing industry. I answered an ad for a small mom-and-pop staffing company and joined the firm. I quickly worked my way through every role in the small organization. After diversifying my skill set, I received a call from a recruiter one day asking if I would be interested in moving to a new company.

. . . .

Their belief in me, even at this early stage in my career, was instrumental in my growth and in my career track.

. . . .

I remember the initial fear I had in taking another risk. Was I ready to go from a small mom-and-pop firm to a large national firm? I took another leap of faith and again, the risk paid off for me, working with a team of brilliant talent, especially my manager, Pam, and helping me to grow into the leader I am today. I moved from a branch manager to a national sales role within three years. I grew from managing a few million dollars to a national $50+ million program.

Risk-taking is central to my core makeup and is one of my top three talents. I have leapt into many new cities and many new career roles without looking back. I wouldn't be where I am without this as one of my top talents, and risk-taking is one of the main reasons I have been able to build and grow Simon Says Give and Simon Says Lead.

Work Ethic/Personal Accountability

The last of my top T's are work ethic and personal accountability. When I reflect on my life, work ethic and accountability are talents and are also part of my personal value system. Perhaps the feeling of being personally responsible and taking accountability for the people and commitments in my life is such a strong, overarching value for me because I felt so abandoned when my mom left her responsibilities and commitments behind in her death. Perhaps accountability is part of my genetic makeup. At any rate, these two things show up over and over in my life and leadership journey.

After my mom died, Dad was working long hours in his corporate role. My older sister, Debbie, had moved home to help out, but she was busy with work and school. The first Thanksgiving after Mom had died, I cooked the entire dinner—I knew how after helping my mom since I had been very little. My dad's expertise in the kitchen was BBQ and I'd help him with the side dishes. One day I had washed dishes, mopped the floor, and helped my younger sister, Susie, with her homework. My dad came home and said, "Thank you." From that moment on, I picked up the slack at home and made sure my little sister was watched after and cared for in a way that Dad couldn't provide. This is the beginning of my value and talent of personal accountability.

Additionally, I started working, babysitting as many jobs as I could fit after school and on the weekends. I saved my money; I had a savings account at the local bank in the nearby shopping mall within walking distance. I had a favorite bank teller and I'd stand in her line to put money in and take money out. I used this money to buy my first pair of Guess designer jeans and my first pair of Nike athletic shoes. Dad gave us one hundred dollars at the beginning of the school season, and anything over and above I wanted or wanted my little sister to have, I purchased on my own. My older sister, Debbie, also made sure we had the school supplies or clothing items we needed. When I turned fifteen, Debbie was the manager of Chop Stick Inn and she got me in there working as a hostess. From that first job, I continued working several jobs all the way through high school and into college. My dad paid my high school tuition; however, I was on my own for everything else and the college costs that followed.

Moving into my career, I quickly saw how the people and organizations I worked for relied on me for my tenacity and personal commitment to make sure we were successful. After I had taken my first vice president role, I was lucky enough to have an executive team that realized the value of bringing in an outside leadership development firm to the organization to help in the field and at headquarters. We partnered with The Ken Blanchard Companies, as it was the premier leadership company, to help us develop leadership capacity.

I worked hard and took all the certifications offered, eager to sharpen my tools as a leader. After training, I was tasked with leading rollouts within the field and back at headquarters. The Ken Blanchard models helped catapult me as a leader and I still use the foundations of these models in every aspect of who I am as a leader today.

One of my favorite examples of the shift and change in how I grew as a leader in my career and as a mother was when Mandi turned four. I wanted to teach her the value of personal accountability and working hard to achieve goals.

Mandi and I made her a "Star Chart." If she could be a "good girl" during the day, she would get a star on her chart. If she got stars every day for a week, she would be rewarded with a Barbie Jeep—something she wanted more than anything in the world. She was good as gold on the first day. On the second and third days, she fell back into her behaviors of not listening and whining to get her way.

On that third night when she was getting ready for bed, I asked her how come she was having a difficult time being good, like the first day of the Star Chart. She cried and said, "I don't know what being a good girl looks like." My four-year-old daughter explained to me, even after my Ken Blanchard training, that I hadn't communicated clear expectations around "being good." I couldn't believe I had missed this in my Star Chart accountability lesson for my daughter. I apologized to Mandi and said, "Of course you wouldn't know what being good looks like because I didn't do my job in explaining the behaviors I am looking for from you."

Mandi and I went straight down to the refrigerator and wrote down the three behaviors we were looking for from her. She exhibited those behaviors in the next week and earned her Barbie Jeep. She still tells this story about learning how to be accountable and work hard to achieve goals. Often in my role as a leader and a mom, I reflect back on the Barbie Jeep when I have a situation where I have to provide direction and support.

The T in the STOP model stands for talents. These are the innate talents you have that are unique to you and how these talents will move you to the next space. Talents are a critical component in the STOP model. My top three talents are relationship building, risk-taking, and work ethic/personal accountability.

Summary of the Second Step in STOP Is T as in Talents

The second step in being *Unstoppable* in our STOP model is to identify the unique talents you bring to the table. Reflect on different moments in your life. How did you move through these times using your unique gifts? Ask someone who knows you well what they believe are your unique talents? Are there times when you haven't been authentic in using your own innate talents? How did that work? Identify your top three talents, the talents you know have helped you bring success in your life moments.

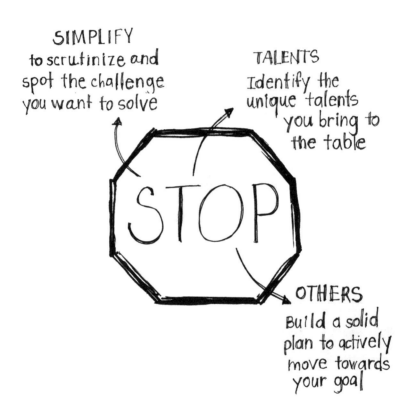

SIMPLIFY
to scrutinize and
spot the challenge
you want to solve

TALENTS
Identify the
unique talents
you bring to
the table

STOP

OTHERS
Build a solid
plan to actively
move towards
your goal

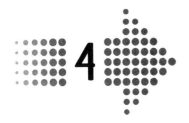

The O Is for Others in the STOP Model

I have talked about relationship building because it is one of my top talents in the STOP model. Relationship building is a central part of who I am and how I have moved into building and growing Simon Says Give and Simon Says Lead. In the STOP model, the O represents others—or how we connect and utilize our relationship resources. After the *Pinnacle Moment* in the kitchen with Mandi and we had decided to move forward with Simon Says Give, I took an inventory of the people in our life and of the support we had from these people to bring our ideas to life. Once I identified the relationships we had in place, I could see the gaps of new relationships I'd need to build.

Looking back over my life, I can see how the people in my life have impacted me and where I am today in both my life and my leadership journey. Each of these relationships has built the foundation for me to move into my current role as CEO of Simon Says Give and Simon Says Lead. Let's take a look at how to identify and build the right people into your life to move you to your *Pinnacle Moment*.

My Family

My parents met at a lake cabin in Balsam Lake, Wisconsin. As a child, we spent many lazy summer days on the lake. After my parents married and had my older sister, my mom had three miscarriages in eight years. They wanted more children and adopted me. Four years later, my mom got pregnant with my little sister. We were officially a family of three daughters.

I was the "middle sister," growing up sandwiched between a significantly older and more mature teenager and the baby of the family. The middle spot wasn't a problem for me with my personality. I'd jump in the room and say, "Hello, I'm here—remember me?" I'm certain the middle position in the family has played a role in how I build relationships and manage my role as a mom and a CEO.

There are some legendary tales about how I treated my little sister and as I share them, I am amazed we have such a deep connection today! When she was a baby, I tipped a big white chest of drawers over on top of her. Luckily, the drawers were out of the dresser at the time and it magically landed so that she was in a drawer opening and wasn't injured. I was only about five years old, and when my mom heard the noise of the crashing chest and ran into the room, she went into shock after she pulled the dresser off my little sister.

Another time, we were jumping on the bed in our parents' room and my two-year-old sister bounced off, falling to the floor and turning blue. My mom almost lost it that day when she shook my sister and she started breathing again. Another trick I would pull would be to make my little sister cry. Then I'd run to my mom crying before my sister could get to her and reverse the story. My mom seemed to believe me every time.

Then there was the time I wrapped a string around her little toe, so tightly that my mom had to take her to the hospital to have the string cut off. I remember after this incident, my dad sat me down in my bedroom. He stood over me and said, "Dina, you are a bully." No one else in my family had ever labeled my behavior in that way. This feedback was a turning point for me.

To be *Unstoppable*, you do have to stop and take a look at your life. What is out of sync in your relationships, and how do you nurture the relationships back to where you desire them to be? I was under ten years old when my dad called my behavior bullying. I didn't realize my relationship with my sister was out of sync at the time. But I did change my behavior with my sister, and to this day, Susie and I have an amazingly strong and unconditional love for each other.

To be *Unstoppable*, you do have to stop and take a look at your life.

My older sister, Debbie, once gave me a piece of advice: "You do not have to do anything you do not want to do in life." I am not completely sure of the context—maybe I was being pressured to do something by my peer group at the time. But that advice has stuck with me all these years. I've used her advice to reflect on my reasons for taking a risk or making a decision. Was I making a personal decision, or was someone forcing me to do something I wasn't comfortable doing? Was I passionate about the decision I was making, and did it feel right for my value system?

Or did I need to walk away from someone or something because it just wasn't working? Being *Unstoppable* means you learn there are moments you have to walk away and change the direction or path. Both my sibling relationships have supported me unconditionally in my life and leadership journey.

Another family "other," or significant person in my life, who helped me arrive where I am today is my father. Growing up, my relationship with my dad was tenuous. We are very different, and yet we are very much alike. My relationship with my dad had, for many years, been out of sync. Before Rich and I moved back to Minnesota, my dad had been diagnosed with Alzheimer's disease. Alzheimer's is prevalent in my father's family genetics, so we weren't surprised. The move back to Minnesota allowed me to prioritize my relationship with my dad and resolve our past.

Dad's favorite quote that sums up his perspective was, "I never have to apologize because I am never wrong." However, in his years with Alzheimer's disease, he relaxed and became much more mellow than he'd been when he was younger. When I came back to Minnesota after being gone for fifteen years, he didn't remember some of the harder times we had experienced together—how he hadn't walked me down the aisle on my wedding day, or how I didn't attend his second wedding. Because of his disease and my desire to rebuild our relationship, we were able to start over and connect in a new way. He became a grandpa that Mandi will remember. We came so far in our relationship, I even gave the eulogy at his funeral.

The O's in your life are constantly changing. People come in and out of your life at different times, and learning how to manage and nurture these relationships is a key to being *Unstoppable*.

My Husband

The biggest O relationship decision that one can make is their life partner. For me, I chose Rich at a young age. Eighteen years later, we are supportive partners with both our daughter and our career lives. We have pushed each other in obtaining a Ph.D. and vice president roles, adopting a daughter, and now bringing to life our daughter's vision for a nonprofit in Simon Says Give. Without our strong partnership, we wouldn't be where we are in our *Unstoppable* journey.

They say you marry your opposite, and that is true with us. Rich and I are very much alike in our beliefs, values, and Midwestern upbringing. When you look at the talents we bring to the world, we are very different. Rich is the smartest person I have ever met. Certainly he had to study some, but he walked away with a Ph.D. in analytical chemistry with ease. If you ever need a lifeline on a game show, you want Rich to be waiting for your call! The talents I bring to the world in our partnership are very different. I probably am not the best lifeline on a game show, but I am an exuberant cheerleader, and I will be the one to get you on the show because I took you to market and landed the gig. I live on the entrepreneurial, creative sales, and marketing spectrum. I am the risk taker who won't let any grass grow under my feet.

Last November, I was upstairs in my office on a conference call—a call that lasted longer than I had expected. Rich was home sick and I could smell the chicken noodle soup he was making on the stove. I walked down the stairs and stood next to the stove. I was stunned and speechless for a moment, which was unlike me. Rich said, "Dina, what happened?"

The words came pouring out: "I just had a call with the Jefferson Awards Foundation and specifically with Sam Beard! He's the co-founder of the Jefferson Awards with Jackie Kennedy!"

Rich said, "Slow down, what?" I pulled up a chair at the table while he ate his chicken soup and explained that the Jefferson Foundation wanted Mandi to be a GlobeChanger and partner with the Jefferson Awards.

I sat back in my chair. I knew this was life-changing for Mandi, for our little nonprofit, for the reach of how we were going to serve and how we could grow. Rich put his spoon down, grabbed my hand—he's not one to mince words—and said, "Wow, this is amazing news. Mandi and Simon Says Give deserve this partnership." The Jefferson Awards Foundation will be instrumental in changing the trajectory of Simon Says Give. With unconditional support, Rich understands the impact this partnership will make and that Mandi and I will be putting a lot of time and energy into this new role. He will participate when and where his talents can help but most importantly, we have his support.

High School Teachers

I wrote for the high school newspaper. I'd wanted to be a journalism major in college. My journalism teacher in high school told me one day after school, "Dina, you could never be a journalist because you would take every story to heart and get too emotional." That comment impacted me in a way that changed the path of my life.

This experience with my journalism teacher is an important lesson in choosing how the others in your life influence your decision-making. You can't always pick the people who surround you in life—I couldn't choose my journalism teacher, nor have I been able to choose the people I've worked with in the past. But these O's influence your life, and how you choose to use their influence over your decision-making is instrumental in your journey.

The O's you can choose to surround yourself with are the most important choices in your life and leadership. Even though

. . . .

You can't always pick the people who surround you in life.

. . . .

I couldn't choose my journalism teacher, I did make choices in relationships with two other high school teachers whom I mentioned previously, Sue Orlowski and Dick Paul. Dick's nickname for me was "Smiles." His nickname for me made the light inside me burn brighter—he can probably be called my first leadership coach. I'd sit in the brown leather chair across from his big administration desk and he'd help me choose college prep classes or lift my spirits if I had been having a bad day. Even after I graduated, I stayed close to both Dick and Sue and visited them at Totino-Grace when I came home from college. They both flew to Dallas to read at my wedding. Coincidentally, the next year Dick and Sue were married and I traveled to northern Minnesota to do a reading at their wedding.

Unfortunately, Dick's life was taken too young, and I was honored to do a reading at his funeral. To this day, I still choose Sue to support my leadership and life journey. She sits on the board of directors as our vice chair for Simon Says Give. These two people are perfect examples of O's whom I've chosen to build my life around and O's who have been invaluable resources. They are examples of how O's have made me be *Unstoppable!*

Leadership

The next O's you need to identify in your life are your leadership O's. Who do you have in your life already that pushes you to where you want to be? Who do you need to add to your life to help you on your leadership journey? Sadly, I hear from a lot of people that they do not feel they have great leaders leading them. They don't have great examples of what "good" leadership looks like. If you find yourself in this situation, there are dynamic leaders out there. Build a strategy to find and recruit dynamic leaders to mentor you. Identify the gaps in your leadership O's. Who do you have around you, and who do you need to recruit?

I have been fortunate to work for two large national staffing firms that had a lot of things in common, including an entrepreneurial spirit and founders who started the business with the values of making a difference in the world while at the same time growing a company. Since my experience in building a relationship with Dick, the vice principal of my high school, I learned to not be afraid to start at the top to build relationships.

In my first corporate role within the staffing industry, I immediately made a strong connection with the founder, Jerry Shaw. I remember the day I had an idea and needed some advice on how to proceed. I picked up the phone and called Jerry. I jumped two levels of leaders to call him that day. At that moment, I didn't have butterflies flitting about in my stomach—I was my authentic self in engaging with the founder—and he answered my call. We started problem solving. I forgot I was talking to the "company founder" and I was able to move forward with my idea. This is the beginning of establishing my core belief that from the very top, it's critical to have strong relationships at every level to move an organization forward.

Thankfully, my direct manager didn't care and actually mentored me with the approach of going directly to Jerry. In building my relationship with Jerry, I found a level of support where he would fly out to my region and drive for two days to see clients and key accounts and have dinner with my team. Our relationship moved from professional support to personal support; he was one of the first people to meet my daughter. The lesson here is even if the O's in your leadership are at the executive level and seem untouchable, reach out directly and see how this relationship could help you grow in your leadership journey.

Summary of the Third Step in STOP Is O as in Others

In the STOP model, the O represents others, or how we connect and utilize our relationship resources. Reflect on your relationships with your siblings, your parents, and your influencers in school and career. How have you built and maintained these relationships? What is out of sync, and what can you do to nurture and lead the relationship to the next level? How have you let the O's you can't choose influence you and your decisions? Who are new O's with whom you want to create relationships to open new doors in your journey?

5

Building a Core Relationship Strategy

I've talked about how identifying the others (O's) in your life can help you move into your *Pinnacle Moment*. For me, this is the most critical aspect of the STOP model and truly the most critical aspect to my life. Everything I have worked through in life has been with someone important—a professional or personal support—at my side. I believe life is meant to be lived with others—life is meant to be messy and meaningful when we creatively work through life's situations together.

Relationships are essentially the most important resource in your life. A plethora of philosophers have analyzed relationships from an economic standpoint. Steven Covey, motivational author, is one of the first to coin the phrase "emotional bank account." When we view relationships from an economic perspective, Covey would say that each O in your life essentially has an emotional bank account. We either put emotional deposits in our O's personal bank accounts or we make emotional withdrawals. In the same vein, the O's in our life also make deposits or withdrawals from our very own emotional bank accounts. The most satisfying relationships have approximately the same amount of deposits and withdrawals (Covey, 2013).

Another way Covey describes the economic benefit of relationships, and the way I prefer to view the core people whom I work with and who are in my network, is as having a "relationship bank account" (Covey, 2013). I either deposit or withdraw from my O's relationship bank accounts. I'm contacted weekly by people, even strangers, and within the first sentence, they have an ask—something they need or want from me. They ask without knowing me or without offering even an idea of how we might partner together in some way. Just last week I met a woman who asked me, "Dina, can you connect me with people from CBS so I can get an interview for my new business?"

I am a person whose first question when I meet someone is, "How can I help you?" This makes me willing to give before I receive. However, when someone has offered or deposited something in my "relationship bank account" first and then asks something of me, I am more likely to help. In viewing relationships as resources, it's important to figure out how you can offer a "give" even before you present an "ask" in return (Fogarty, 2013). Or ask yourself, "Am I making a relationship deposit or a relationship withdrawal, and how can I ensure I'm not withdrawing more than I'm depositing?"

Four Tiers of Strategic Relationships

Building and implementing a relationship strategy is essential in the STOP model (Neitlich, 2005). Based on the economic theory of relationships, you will be much more successful when you learn to evaluate the key relationships you have in your life. Then, strategically focus effectively on those relationships that offer the most mutually satisfying economic benefit to reaching your goals or moving to your *Pinnacle Moments* and being *Unstoppable*.

TIER ONE: INNER CIRCLE O RELATIONSHIPS

The way I define my Inner Circle of trusted advisors is how we fit together with our personality styles, our talents and gifts, and our shared value system (Schwartz, 2012; Neitlich, 2005). For example, my Inner Circle is made up of a close peer group of like-minded people with some of the same gifts and some very different gifts and talents. The thing we have in common is a shared value system. My Inner Circle is my group, or "tribe," and it has helped me move to my *Pinnacle Moment* and my most authentic self.

Finding your Inner Circle of O's is critical to the STOP model. As you've read about some of the people whom I've described, you may have a good idea of those who are in my Inner Circle—my tribe, the cast of characters with whom I spend quality time. When I refer to "like-minded," I don't mean those who will have the same answers or think in the same way I do. I mean like-minded in the core values and the belief in our relationship to come to the table to work through the problems we have to solve.

. . . .

My Inner Circle is my group, or "tribe," and it has helped me move to my *Pinnacle Moment* and my most authentic self.

. . . .

My Inner Circle is extremely fluid and is made of more than just a few people. The *Unstoppable* relationships with people in my personal and professional life that support me unconditionally receive the very same from me in return. We challenge each other's thinking in a healthy and constructive way because there is the ultimate confidence in our motives. My Inner Circle O relationships in the STOP model are a group of people whom I add to on a continual basis.

One of my favorite stories in adding relationships to my Inner Circle is Lou Abramowski and the first time I met him. I had been meeting with Jeff Brown at a cooperative workspace in downtown Minneapolis by the name of CoCo, and Jeff had told me I should meet this young and refreshing entrepreneur who was in a busy and central camp at CoCo. When I met Lou for the first time, I hugged him before we shook hands. We had an immediate connection and I was completely inspired by what I had been told about him. After a couple meetings with Lou, we found a project to work on together and this is when he became a core relationship in my Inner Circle. Lou serves on the board of Simon Says Give and is a partner in Simon Says Lead. He has taught me more about technology and social marketing than he probably ever thought I had the mental capacity to learn.

The reason Lou fits perfectly in my Inner Circle is because he and I bring very different skill sets to life in our personal and professional spaces. However, we have mutual trust and admiration to work extremely hard with and for each other because we celebrate the team we make. Lou has an amazing network and has accomplished (and will continue to accomplish) things in his professional life. When he talks about the work we do within Simon Says Give and Simon Says Lead, I smile. He is so inspired by the work we are doing, which I find remarkable based on the work he does on a daily basis outside of our partnership. This is the type of O I strategically look for to build into my Inner Circle of relationships.

There are moments when I sit in a room full of people in awe and wonder how I became so lucky in life to be collaborating with my core group of Inner Circle O's. I am completely awed when I see my young daughter has been afforded the opportunity to be sitting at the same table, and really won't understand until she's many years older the contribution these business professionals have made to the world. Mandi has been exposed to an amazing Inner Circle of leaders since the very day my former boss Jerry Shaw sat on my living room couch and held her in his arms.

To this day, Mandi still talks about how she earned her Barbie Jeep from her Star Chart and how Pete Nolfo, one of my developers in the Northeast, was at our house helping her understand how to win. Even at eight years old, Mandi was invited to the board room table at Rich's company meeting with senior executives to pitch why this large company in the Twin Cities needed to be involved with Simon Says Give. My daughter, at a very young age, also understands the importance of building a strong network of Inner Circle O relationships.

Another relationship I've talked about in my Inner Circle is Jeffrey Hayzlett. I met Jeffrey in Hollywood at a speakers and authors event in May 2011. I received an invitation via LinkedIn from Jeffrey inviting me to a dinner event in October 2011. If Jeffrey was inviting me to a dinner, I was going to be there. As this Inner Circle relationship has continued, he has always watched out for opportunities for me to have a seat at the table, including his C-Suite Conference table and the C-Suite Book Club that inspired this book.

Sitting right across the table from me at the dinner Jeffrey had invited me to in October 2011 was Jeff Brown. Three years later, Jeff is one of my most trusted advisers. He sits on the Simon Says Give board and is a partner in Simon Says Lead. Jeff has pushed me to not only think big but also do big, and how to take that big thinking and put it into *Unstoppable* action. This is the way to strategically build a core Inner Circle of O's—one relationship leads to another.

. . . .

This is the way to strategically build a core Inner Circle of O's—one relationship leads to another.

. . . .

In a typical week, Jeff calls me around nine a.m. on a Monday or Tuesday to check in with me. One early morning, he didn't hear sunshine in my voice. He asked me, "What's wrong, Dina?" When I shared with him the problem, he said, "Dina, you know the answer. You know what to do." He reframed the problem in a way I hadn't yet. His perspective, something so simple, and something I couldn't see without his help, is all I needed that day. I said to Jeff, "Thank you for talking me off the ceiling!"

Having an Inner Circle allows you to have a safe sounding board and to lean on the creative insight and perspectives of trusted advisors. That day, I relied on sharing my problem with one of my Inner Circle O's and in less than a five-minute conversation, Jeff and I had solved the problem. I was able to move to resolution in a meaningful way.

I believe my philosophy to serve and put my Inner Circle first is a characteristic that has grown out of being an adopted child. There is a facet of my personality that has a huge desire to be a "people pleaser." A little piece that stuck with me from my adoption is the fearful thought that I might be given back. My "people pleaser" desire may be a result of being an adopted child; however, this experience has led me to build my relationship strategy of giving and has become a huge part of who I am today.

In sum, I may be a little different than most people in terms of being so fluid with people in my Inner Circle. Much of the reason I have the ability to build teams around me is because of my talent for relationship building and understanding the concept of the relationship bank account, or my "How can I help you?" motto. I work day and night for the people in my Inner Circle—I work at all costs to prevent my relationships from getting out of sync in terms of taking more out of the account than I have given. I lean in with gratitude and a "How can I serve?" attitude before I ask for the help I might need. A critical component to a relationship strategy is to build your Inner Circle and identify the right O's to mutually support you in the STOP model to help you move toward your *Pinnacle Moments*!

TIER TWO: CATALYST O RELATIONSHIPS

Catalyst O's are the next important ingredient to your relationship strategy (Schwartz, 2012; Fogarty, 2013). This is a group of people who have both the mutual respect and the mutual intentions to support each other in endeavors. At any time, Catalysts may move into the Inner Circle once the level of trust and intimacy has moved past the level of influencing success only.

Since Catalyst O's have the potential to move to Inner Circle O's, it's critical to put effort into growing and expanding your Catalyst O network. Identifying your Catalyst O's might be a little tricky. Some people find networking and adding mutually beneficial connections an intimidating and daunting task. Networking is something I thrive on and a talent I have, therefore I realize this is not easy for everyone. When you are looking to connect with Catalyst O's, one thing to consider is, "Do these O's have a well-connected or large social network?" What does their impact seem to be on others in this Catalyst group? Are these potential Catalyst O's trendsetters in your space? Are these Catalyst O's active within the community, and do they have diverse interests? Does this Catalyst O fill a talent gap, something I need that I don't have to move forward?

When identifying who I can be a Catalyst for, and who might be a Catalyst for me, I have these potential O people on my radar and I start watching for them to show up in my life. I will look to see what they are up to from time to time, and I might even set up a Google alert for their company or their name. There have been times when people in this arena have won awards or have been recognized for their contribution, and I will send a note or other personal communication to help celebrate with them. In this way, I start to build a supportive rapport with my potential Catalyst O's.

For my Catalyst O relationships, I am on the lookout for any connection or synergy of support that I can offer in moving our business relationship forward. I am vigilant in finding out as much as I can about Catalyst O's business and goals. The way we make deposits and withdrawals from one another's relationship bank accounts is by making connections and referrals, and promoting each other in our business endeavors. We work in conjunction for our mutual success.

A good example of one of my strong Catalyst O's is Darin Lynch. Darin and I were brought together to collaborate with Mandi to build our website for Simon Says Give. We had a strong connection immediately as we shared some of the same business goals, and we became Catalyst O's for one another. Darin and I have continued to support and refer business back and forth to each other over the past few years. I'm not sure how many dollars in business or clients I have referred to Darin, or how much he has referred work to me, but we are very committed to helping each other succeed.

Recently, we were nominated for a big award in the Minnesota area, the ACG BOLD Awards. I wasn't shocked to find out

Darin was the one who nominated Simon Says Give. Simon Says Give gained many strategic partners due to this award nomination and recognition. Darin is an example of someone who is both an Inner Circle and a Catalyst O in my relationship strategy. He is fluid in being both a Catalyst O and a strategic partner with us at Simon Says Give, and as being part of my Inner Circle of trusted advisors.

TIER THREE: CLOSE COMMUNITY O RELATIONSHIPS

The Close Community Others is your bigger network, or groups with similar value-based political, social, charitable, or economic perspectives (Schwartz, 2012). The reason it's important to identify your Close Community O's is because Catalyst O's have potential to move to your Inner Circle—likewise, Close Community O's may move into Catalyst O relationships. These strategic relationships allow for fluidity in building stronger connections to move into your *Pinnacle Moment*.

I am strategic and search for connections where we can work together for the greater good. I have spent my life collecting friends and people along my journey. My relationship strategy is the foundation of who I am in my talents in the STOP model, and is the ultimate key to my success in business and working through life situations in identifying the others in the STOP model. Not all of my relationships, or O's, have been easy. Again, some of the most beneficial ones have been the hardest ones to work through to the other side.

. . . .

I have spent my life collecting friends
and people along my journey.

. . . .

I am intentionally purposeful in building strategic relationships with my Close Community O's. For example, I determine how often I connect with my different types of relationships. I recently received a reference call from someone who used to work with me in California over nine years ago. I consider her to be in my Close Community of relationships, and I am able to be a viable reference for her because we have stayed connected. We may only talk live once a year, but we are connected via many channels. If she ever needed me or I needed her, we are in one another's Close Community network where we can easily pick up where we left our relationship.

Another way you can leverage your Close Community of relationships is by asking for not only professional but also personal help. When we knew that we were going to adopt, I shared our plans in our Christmas letter that year. After sharing our personal story within our Close Community O's, we had several calls from people, our friends and others, only a few days later with stories they wanted to share. Many offered any help we may need in our adoption endeavor. These stories helped support us on our journey. This is the power of communicating and sharing your story with your Close Community O's—what may transpire to help you move to your *Pinnacle Moment* can only be replicated by maintaining these close relationships.

TIER FOUR: EXTENDED COMMUNITY O RELATIONSHIPS

The last strategic relationships of others are the Extended Community O's (Schwartz, 2012). The Extended Community is the community that doesn't know you well and doesn't have a direct influence on your success. Analyze the social community of LinkedIn or Twitter for an example of your Extended Community. There may be times when you have walked into a room and have seen someone and feel as if you have met them before. When you talk, you find out you are connected within the same social media networks. "Follow to be followed" by those whom you feel are in a space you want to be. This is the start of an Extended Community relationship. This is a tactical example of how you begin to build your strategic community network toward your goals. Where do you want to be and whom do you want to know about you in that space?

I view the Extended Community as something like your extended family. This group may be a group of people you only see every ten years during family reunions, however the connection remains—there is still a tie between you! The Extended Community works in the same way. One connection leads to another connection and before you know it, you will be matching people with people who can help each other.

About a year ago, I was asked to go to a networking event through our business journal, and I said, "Yes!" The night of the event, the drive was terrible—thick snowflakes and rush-hour traffic. I almost turned my car around three times to head back home. Finally, I arrived at the event, and I connected with someone who provided a huge partnership in business. Later that night, I walked happily in the dark back to my snowed-in car parked miles away up on a hill. I could have turned the car around and gone home earlier that evening. However, I was invested in being there to support the person who extended the invitation, and I had received, in return for my drive-time investment, a business opportunity that proved to be huge for us.

Summary of the Four Tiers of Relationships

There are four categories in the relationship strategy as you look at your network of others: Inner Circle, Catalyst, Close, and Extended Community. We used all four types of relationships as we launched Simon Says Lead. We identified a few people in the Inner Circle and Catalyst roles who were at our launch parties, and who agreed to speak at our monthly events. Our take-to-market strategy of going in and working with leaders and businesses to help them solve their problems came to be because we have a vast Close and Extended Community of relationships. From our Inner Circle to our Catalyst circle to the Community circle—a group of people rich in talents—we are able to leverage our strategic relationships to move us forward. The time and effort it takes to build people in the four strategic relationship areas is worth the effort. When you find meaningful ways of working on projects together, it can be the key to moving you into your *Pinnacle Moment*.

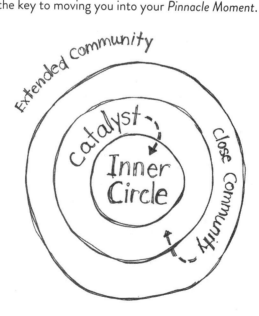

70/20/10: Time Spent with Your Network of Relationships

A relationship strategy allows you to identify the four types of O relationships you have in your life. Then we strategically focus our time on our relationships that bring us closer to becoming who we want to be—*Unstoppable!*

The way I spend time in my relationship strategy is 70/20/10. I spend 70 percent of my time on my Inner Circle relationships. I spend about 20 percent of my time on Catalysts, and 10 percent on Close Community and Extended Community. Chunking your time in this way allows you to systematically spend the biggest amount of time on the most meaningful relationships (Inner Circle and Catalyst) and less time on the relationships that you aren't working with as closely (Close and Extended Community).

The way I use my relationship strategy is to keep track of time I spend on each relationship in my Inner Circle O's, my Catalyst O's, my Close Community O's, and my Extended Community O's. I determine how often I am connecting with the relationships in each area, and make note of what the strategic connections are and business purposes we may have in working together.

In building a relationship strategy, the first step is taking the time to identify who I have in each area of the relationships (Inner Circle, Catalyst, Close, and Extended Community) and who is on the radar for becoming a possible strategic relationship. Then, I build a relationship strategy around how often I need to

. . . .

The way I use my relationship strategy is to keep track of time I spend on each relationship.

. . . .

be talking to them and how and when I provide value or deposit something into the relationship account. When you've identified someone who is a Close Community O and you want to move him or her into a Catalyst O, it is important to be creative in figuring out how you can help him or her. That creativity will determine how long it will take before they become a Catalyst O.

A good rule of thumb to follow in deciding when to move a relationship to the next level is after you have offered one or two relationship deposits—either in offering some relevant industry knowledge/information or providing connections or business referrals. After I bring value a couple of times, I am then in a position to find out how we can make the relationship meaningful and purposeful for both of us. It sounds so simple, but if we forget to be purposeful about building strategic and meaningful others (O's) in the STOP model, we likely won't move to *Unstoppable.*

TIME SPENT WITH MY INNER CIRCLE O'S

For example, the way I organize my time on my Inner Circle is to spend the majority of my time on these O relationships, which are my team from Simon Says Give and other close-working partnerships. These relationships are the ones that are most mutually beneficial for moving us both forward in being *Unstoppable* and are most likely the people I am collaborating and working with on a regular basis.

However, I do have some Inner Circle O's whom I only see in person or talk to on a quarterly basis. The reason these relationships are still considered Inner Circle is because we have built a foundation of deep mutual trust and respect in prior life situations. Essentially, that lifeline Inner Circle relationship has enough banked or deposited in the relationship account to be pulled out in emergency situations based on our past of working together and supporting each other.

The Inner Circle—both the people I work with on a daily basis and the people who are the lifeline Inner Circle of my world—know who they are because I am not frugal in communicating this fact to them. Perhaps because of my experiences of losing so many people in my life, I operate using open communication. I don't mince words in telling those who are important to me that they are—and I do so as often as I can! In my relationship strategy, I think of chunking at least 70 percent of my time making deposits in the relationship bank accounts of and supporting my Inner Circle in what they need to be *Unstoppable*.

Jim Johnson is someone who has moved through my relationship strategy and network. He started in my Close Community, then became a Catalyst, and is now an Inner Circle O and someone I consider as close as a brother. Jim and I just had a meeting with our Simon Says Give team and we both walked away with action items of deposits in each of our relationship bank accounts. He has people whom he is going to introduce me to, and I have a list of things I can do for him. When we come together to collaborate, we both walk away with mutually beneficial ways in which we can help each other grow. I invest a lot of time into my relationship with Jim because anything that comes out of this relationship—a connection or partnership lead—is one that will likely end up being of significant value. The relationship with Jim, and the time I invest, almost 100 percent of the time results in something beneficial to move me forward.

When I was Jim's vice president attending the annual leadership awards, my co-worker Amy Redmond and I knew he was going to hit the Chairman's Club Award level for the first time. We were standing at the bottom of the stage before he walked up to the red carpet. The tears started streaming down our faces, because the dedication of hard work he and his team had put in to achieve this level of success was so inspiring to us. Celebrating the success of Inner Circle O's—celebrating the spirit of the relationship—can be some of the most rewarding moments in life. This is a prime example of how Inner Circle O's support each other and are an instrumental component in the STOP model.

TIME SPENT WITH MY CATALYST O'S

When organizing my time on my Catalyst O's in my relationship strategy, I consider these people to be on my radar. I learn what I can about what's going on in their world and how I can help. I want them to know appropriately what's going on in my world, because after making relationship deposits, I, in turn, am counting on my Catalysts to reciprocate these deposits in the form of helping me in my endeavors. Again, I operate from the space that most people want to help each other—they just need to know what is needed. If we are doing our job of being creative—asking the right questions and listening to the answers—then we have the right information about the Catalyst O's goals to help them and vice versa. Our Catalyst relationships must be mutually beneficial, and this is what I like to call an *Unstoppable* win-win.

The time I spend with my Catalyst O's is approximately 20 percent. The way I communicate with them is less personal than my Inner Circle O's, as I choose the phone or in-person

. . . .

Our Catalyst relationships must be mutually beneficial, and this is what I like to call an *Unstoppable* win-win.

. . . .

conversations with my Inner Circle O's 70 percent of the time. However, for my Catalyst relationships, I send personal notes to congratulate or thank them. I also use social media channels to invite them to events or send relevant articles and links that may be beneficial to their business. Additionally, I connect them with people I meet, and I do make sure I touch base with a personal call or face-to-face conversation on a quarterly basis.

TIME SPENT WITH MY CLOSE AND EXTENDED COMMUNITY

My relationship strategy has four key areas. I am looking at identifying people in my Close and Extended Community who can move into Catalyst or Inner Circle tiers. It may seem unimportant to strategically identify the Close and Extended Community O's because they are not impacting and influencing your daily life, or getting you to be *Unstoppable* in this moment. I maintain this may be why so many people don't succeed in reaching their goals, because they have limited their relationship strategy to their Inner Circle and maybe just make it to the Catalyst relationships. This is a shallow and shortsighted way of viewing relationship strategy and will at some point limit your success.

For example, let's say you have thousands of LinkedIn connections. These connections are not categorized (Inner Circle, Catalyst, Close, or Extended Community) in your relationship strategy. However, these are connections that can easily become part of your relationship strategy. Take the people in your LinkedIn network and put them into a spreadsheet. This tactile strategy will help you quickly identify whom the people are you need to build into your Close and Extended Community. Once you've identified people in your Close and Extended Community relationship categories, determine how you can connect with them in a meaningful way.

A good rule of thumb for the time you spend on Close and Extended Community relationships is about 10 percent. There are ways to communicate and educate the relationships you've identified in these groups that don't take much time. But when you are ready to connect in a deeper way, the knowledge piece—who you are and how you do what you do—is already in place. For example, the way I keep my Close and Extended Community educated and up-to-date with Simon Says Give and Simon Says Lead is to send out email campaigns and occasionally personal notes. I also communicate with them through social media channels and networking groups.

The Close and Extended Community is an important—and often missed—network of O's in a relationship strategy. Having these relationships O's and a communication plan for these O's in place is important in the STOP model.

Summary of Building a Core Relationship Strategy

Building and implementing a relationship strategy is essential in the STOP model. Identifying the different types of relationships is the first step in this strategy. The types of relationships are as follows: Inner Circle O's, Catalyst O's, Close Community O's, and Extended Community O's. Based on the economic theory of relationships, you will be much more successful when you think about depositing in your O's "relationship bank accounts" and identifying creative ways to help them in reaching their goals.

Building and implementing your relationship strategy is critical in reaching your goals.

The final piece in implementing a relationships strategy is the amount of time spent on each type of relationship. I use the 70/20/10 rule: 70 percent of my time with my Inner Circle relationships, 20 percent on my Catalyst relationships, and 10 percent on my Close and Extended Community. Building and implementing your relationship strategy is critical in reaching your goals or moving you toward your *Pinnacle Moments* and being *Unstoppable*.

Reflect on how to build your relationship strategy. Who is in your Inner Circle? Who else do you need in this Inner Circle? Who are your Catalyst O's? How do you view your relationship investments, and how do you make relationship bank account deposits and withdrawals? How much time are you spending with your Inner Circle and your Catalyst O's? Who is in your Close and Extended Community? How are you communicating to these core relationships in your life?

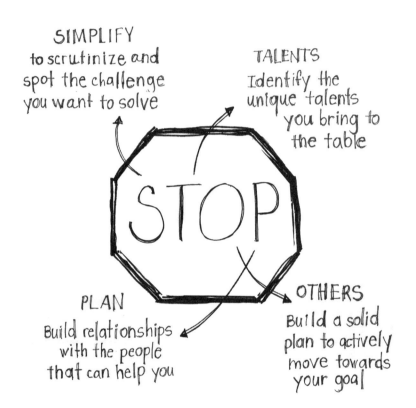

SIMPLIFY
to scrutinize and
spot the challenge
you want to solve

TALENTS
Identify the
unique talents
you bring to
the table

STOP

PLAN
Build relationships
with the people
that can help you

OTHERS
Build a solid
plan to actively
move towards
your goal

6

The P Is for Plan in the STOP Model

The P in the STOP model stands for plan. Now you've completed the first three steps in the STOP model: (1) Simplified to understand what you want to solve; (2) Identified the top three talents you have to help you solve this problem or challenge; and (3) Identified the others or relationships you currently have in your life and recognized the new relationships you need to build. This brings us to the last step in the STOP model. The P step is all about building a solid plan that will help to actively move you toward your goal. It's time to plan for your *Pinnacle Moment*!

I look back now, four years later, after quitting my dream vice president job and the salary I was making. I've been asked if I have regrets and I can honestly say, "No." I remember the moment in a tan hotel bathroom, in a city two thousand miles from my family, when I looked in the mirror and said, "I am done." I needed time to simplify—slow down and find clarity.

When Mandi had come into my life, I wasn't ready to make a career change. At that point, I wanted to work really hard to have a career and have a great relationship with my child. I wanted to be a working mom. I wanted to be the best mom I could be and still retain my identity as a larger-than-life businessperson. For me during that time in my life, happiness was having a team of people around me working on something I valued as important work. I believed if my daughter ever resented the fact that I worked, I'd explain to her why I chose to do what I did and she would appreciate and be proud of me. I felt confident when Mandi looked back on her childhood that she would say, "My mom showed me how to be a strong and independent woman. She showed me every day how important I was to her by doing what she loved and being there for me, too."

I traveled 70 percent of my time for the first seven years of her life. After those years, I came to the moment in my life when I simplified to find clarity by leaving the job and lifestyle I had strived so hard to attain. In those quiet, simplified moments of quality time with my daughter, I discovered that I didn't want to go back to a heavy travel schedule and the rigors of corporate life. Mandi was my one and only daughter. She is what I dreamt about since I was twelve. Time goes by so fast and I am determined to enjoy every moment I can with her.

The journey I have been on the past four years truly has been the richest of them all thus far in my life, both personally and professionally. I quit without having another job lined up, which does not seem very planful and something very unlike me. I have been working since I was fifteen years old. Bringing in a paycheck was pretty important to me and to my family.

The P in Planning for Simon Says Give

We had a recent situation where an executive asked our Simon Says Give team, "What are your goals?" The people on our team chuckled at her question. Our philosophy is truly "The sky's the limit!" There are times when you can over-plan for things. Analysis paralysis. From the early stages of my career, I have been taught to have goals. As a sales professional and leader, I have, for several years, used the P in the STOP model to set my goals. When we set out to plan for our first year of Simon Says Give, we were unsure of what to plan for. We had no idea of what was possible. We took a stab and set hard-to-achieve goals.

Somehow in the first year, we reached each goal we had set. The second year, we set new goals, and they were big ones. Our board laughed and said, "Dina, we aren't going to tell you we can't hit these goals. If we put them out there, we will do everything to hit them—and most likely do just that."

Our corporate sponsors have been extraordinary and a testimony to the value of our P for plan. As I mentioned earlier, Jim Johnson is Mandi's co-founder of High Five for Supplies. Jim and his team continue to be our partners in the High Five for Supplies, with hundreds of Jim's clients engaging in the mission. Jim is a prime example of plan in the STOP model. When we shared with Amy Grove—Simon Says Give's operational partner and the heart and soul behind the High Five for Supplies movement—that we were going from one thousand kids supported in 2013 to ten thousand kids supported in 2014, she blinked several times at me, and then smacked her hand on the table and said, "Sign me up! I know now that we've said it, it will happen! I am in 500 percent." This year, when we told her five states and fifty thousand kids for 2015, she's asking, "Why not more kids and more states?"

Another pivotal planning moment for Simon Says Give happened almost accidentally, and yet became instrumental in the overall planning for our nonprofit. In February 2013, I was asked to do a Pecha Kucha presentation—a Japanese presentation model where the speaker has twenty slides without even one word, only photographs, and the speaker has only twenty seconds to talk about each slide. The pictures I chose described my vision and plan for Simon Says Give.

Typically, I am not a script girl—I just talk—so I was panicked and almost stopped in my tracks. I had to plan what I was going to say for each slide, and I had only twenty seconds to talk for each slide. I walked into a room filled with 150 influential business people in the Twin Cities and I grabbed my rock, Jeff Brown, and said, "Honestly, the slide will move in twenty seconds even if I'm not ready for it to move. I think I need to read from my timed script, which then will totally throw me off and I think I might just pass out right now!"

He laughed and said, "Dina, you've planned and prepared for this presentation—who knows your vision better than you?" Out of the seven speakers that day, I was last to present. Jeff was right (as usual): I did plan for this presentation on my vision. This Pecha Kucha presentation process forced me to find clarity in communicating my vision and plans for Simon Says Give and became pivotal in communicating this vision. At the end of my Pecha Kucha presentation, Jeff Prouty, a Minnesota leadership guru, walked up to me and asked if Mandi would ever speak at one of his monthly Jammin Sessions. Mandi enthusiastically agreed, and we were both honored to do a mother-daughter duo presentation for Jeff. That day in February 2013, we planned and scheduled an event that took place in August 2014. This is the beginning of a series of requests for Mandi to share her story.

From year one to just past year two, we grew the entity to one that was supporting more than ten thousand children in some fashion. We conducted hundreds of birthday celebrations each year and supported over ten thousand kids with back-to-school readiness. Our budget went from $0 to over $1,000,000 moving into our third year.

At the end of each week, I send a "board update" with the goal of sharing the top three things that happened this week and the top three things I need help on from the team. There hasn't been a week when it hasn't been exciting to sit down at the computer to write that email. Typically there are five to ten amazing things to share and maybe only one or two things we need help on, because we have a vision and a plan, and we commit to completing the plan! If we need an office space, an office space appears. When we needed office furniture to fill that office space, a furniture company in town donated our entire office suite.

When we needed a media partner to share our story to help us reach our goals, our Minnesota-based CBS station WCCO partnered with us through their Accomplish Minnesota programming and featured Simon Says Give all summer. The media partnership led to hundreds of new donors and some amazing new corporate sponsors and relationships. These partnerships will take us into the next phase of the journey. At age eleven, Mandi has a board of directors that could run a $10 billion company. Every day something exciting is put in our path. You know you are on the right path when extraordinary people and situations present themselves along your *Unstoppable* journey.

We set monthly, quarterly, and annual goals. For Simon Says Give, we have milestones and a strategic plan that goes through 2022, our ten-year anniversary. We are fluid in our planning. When we do our status meetings, if we determine we are way off target in either direction, we shift and refocus. Each month our organization looks different than it did the month prior; therefore, we have to be flexible in our planning and our use of resources. We are focused with clarity on the end in mind. We prioritize on daily and weekly deliverables that all add up at the end of the year.

Critics

One aspect of Simon Says Give that I didn't plan for, and one that has taken me quite by surprise, are the critics in the world. I moved from receiving feedback from the sidelines like, "Why did you want to be a mom if you're traveling for work?" to "What are you doing supporting an eight-year-old's dream to this level?" At age eleven, Mandi can walk onto a live broadcast interview and handle it like a pro. Therefore, she is often called upon to do so and is in the spotlight. To the critics it appears we are supporting her to only have her in the spotlight. Oh, the stones we throw.

As a mom, I am supporting my daughter and her larger-than-life dream to save the world and making some amazing progress in supporting others. As a professional, I am using all my skills, capabilities, and focus for a greater good! We are coaching other nonprofits using our model and success and are only in year two of operation. We put our business hats on and we went to work not knowing we were trailblazing. As a little girl who lost her mom around Mandi's age, I am honored to be working with my daughter—and I am certain there are angels very hard at work in this entire process.

The full-circle moment goes back to the story of how I came into this world and how Mandi came into the world, and our journey to find each other. If together we were meant to be *Unstoppable*, *Unstoppable* is what we will be. When Mandi goes to school each day, school is school—the place she goes to learn and the place that has developed her spirit and her skills to be doing what she wants to be when she grows into an adult. Her school provides her with the four walls where she can be whoever she wants to be and to learn, grow, and explore. She doesn't have to talk or think about Simon Says Give—she can just be a kid.

. . . .

If together we were meant to be *Unstoppable*, *Unstoppable* is what we will be.

. . . .

Mandi will grow up and do anything in the world she is compelled to try. By the time she goes to college, she will have a multi-million-dollar global nonprofit entity that she can decide what she wants to do with. She may very much decide to walk away from Simon Says Give, and we have a plan B and plan C prepared should this time come. It is her choice. At age eleven, does she know the significance of what she has worked to build? I believe she does, and she has a team of twenty people around her who understand and who will work hard on her behalf and make sure she is still a kid.

The P in Planning for Simon Says Lead

I believe the best way to set up a nonprofit is to have a for-profit company that supports the nonprofit. Almost from day one, Jeff and I have been dreaming about what that would look like for Simon Says Give. Since we began in 2011, we had talked with our friend Barbara Hensley, the founder of the Hope Chest for Breast Cancer. Barbara pioneered the for-profit to nonprofit model fifteen years ago with her for-profit retail shops that feed into the nonprofit foundation. We talked about the trend in the one-for-one business model—buy a birthday party and get a birthday party donated—however, we didn't want to go into the retail business of only providing birthday celebrations.

With my corporate background in staffing and coaching people and teams, Simon Says Lead is a natural fit for the nonprofit and for-profit business model. Simon Says Lead is set up as a benefit corporation to feed a percentage of the profits to Simon Says Give. This will allow us to grow the nonprofit while we continue to grow the for-profit. We will take our courage and our *Unstoppable* natures to replicate the results we have seen thus far on the nonprofit side to the for-profit side.

Simon Says Lead (and the entire business model that is developing out of the last name Simon) will be dedicated to growing leaders at all levels. Grooming Mandi and her friends who serve with Simon Says Give is grooming our next generation of leaders. Growing leaders at Fortune 100 companies and their teams through transformation of their greatest business challenges is growing leaders at every level. Our strategy is one where we want to hear about business challenges and help leaders solve them. We will facilitate putting the STOP model to the test. After we diagnose the true challenges the leadership team is trying to solve, we can create and present solutions. Those solutions might require bringing others to the table, as our team has solid relationship strategies and global talent. The best of the best are called to the table—we have a pretty amazing business proposition to solve the biggest challenges business leaders face.

Our vision board for Simon Says Lead has an office in Minneapolis, an office in San Francisco, and some day New York City (or we might even be in D.C. with Mandi's GlobeChanger role). We believe we have a niche in generational leadership. With our experience on the Simon Says Give side of the house, we have board meetings with people ages eleven to sixty-five. We have learned that the younger you are, the more you actually bring to the party! We will be offering, through Simon Says Lead, a Rolodex of amazing kids and talent who see the future and will help us grown-ups see that it happens!

We have board meetings with people ages eleven to sixty-five.

As we set out to plan for Simon Says Lead, a few things for our go-to-market strategy fell into place with our national network of partners. My co-collaborator Amy Grove comes from an "abundance mentality" and in launching Simon Says Lead, we asked ourselves the question, "How do we get our network of others together to communicate what we're doing?" We decided to build something like a TED Talk—a co-branding and co-marketing speaker event. The logistics for our Simon Says Lead Speaker Series fell into place quickly. One of the partners I've done strategic coaching with, Bridgewater Bank, hosted the location. The speakers we reached out to immediately locked in dates and we were *Unstoppably* off to market. This is a testimony to the relationship strategy and how we put the STOP model to work in a fluid way within our own business.

The STOP model, and how it has lived out in my personal and professional life, continues to be a focus on a daily basis. We have worked to create the Unstoppable You coaching process, the Unstoppable Team coaching process, and the Unstoppable Organization coaching process. This core curriculum takes individuals, teams, and organizations through this STOP model. We take the business problems that a person or company has through the simplifying to solve step to scrutinize the real problems or challenges. Then we facilitate the talents step and allow the person, team, or company to identify the top talents they have to solve this problem. Moving them through the others evaluates whom they have on their team or in their network that they can bring to the table. This is where we also come to the table as a partner to share our relationships to fill the gaps. The others in our STOP model, our relationship strategy, is one of our core business differentiators because we have a network of Inner Circle, Catalyst, and Close and Extended Community that we can tap to bring to the table and help our clients through the process! Then last but not least, we help the individual, team, or organization put a meaningful plan together with actions and accountability to move forward to their *Pinnacle Moment.*

Summary of the Final Step in STOP Is P as in Plan

The P in the STOP model stands for plan. The P is the culmination of the first three steps in STOP. You've completed the first three steps in the STOP model: (1) Simplified to understand what you want to solve; (2) Identified the top three talents you have to help you solve this problem or challenge; and (3) Identified the others or relationships you currently have in your life and recognized the new relationships you need to build. The P step in the STOP model is the solid plan of action you need to make to move on toward your *Pinnacle Moment.*

Reflect on the O's you will need to help you build your plan. What are the obstacles you will have to overcome to put this plan in place? How do your talents play into the plan? Where do your O's come in to support you with the plan? Have you identified the specific and tangible goals in your plan?

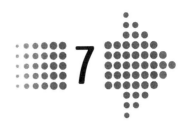

Putting the STOP in *Unstoppable* and How to Make It Simple

In my leadership and life journey, building up to my recent moment of clarity to help start Simon Says Give and Simon Says Lead, we used the STOP model to gain clarity of purpose toward moving along an *Unstoppable* journey. In the un-STOP-pable model, we have pulled out the acronym STOP. The STOP model is a simple method to show you how to tap into your *Pinnacle Moment* of clarity in your life and move toward *Unstoppable*.

THE FIRST STEP IN STOP IS S AS IN SIMPLIFY TO SOLVE

As I've shared, the first step in being *Unstoppable* in our STOP model is to simplify to scrutinize and spot the challenges you want to solve. Reflect on different moments in your life. How did you simplify to block out the noise to find the clarity to solve your challenge? Are there times when you didn't simplify and perhaps missed a *Pinnacle Moment*? How can you implement what it means for you to simplify to solve and find clarity in your life moments?

THE SECOND STEP IN STOP IS T AS IN TALENTS

The second step in being *Unstoppable* in our STOP model is to identify the unique talents you bring to the table. The T in the STOP model stands for talents: the innate talents you have that are personally unique to you and how these talents will move you to the next space. Talents are a critical component in the STOP model. My top three talents are relationship building, risk-taking, and work ethic/personal accountability.

Reflect on different moments in your life. How did you move through these times using your unique gifts? Ask someone who knows you well what they believe are your unique talents. Are there times when you haven't been authentic in using your own innate talents? How did that work? Work with a coach to work through the exploration of your journey to help identify characteristics that continue to show up in your life. There is a world of personality evaluations and assessments that can also help paint a picture of your unique talents. Identify your top three talents that you know have helped you bring success in your life moments.

THE THIRD STEP IN STOP IS O AS IN OTHERS

I have talked about relationship building because it is one of my top talents in the STOP model and is a central part of who I am and how I have moved into building and growing Simon Says Give and Simon Says Lead. In the STOP model, the O represents others, or how we connect and utilize our relationship resources. After the moment in the kitchen with Mandi, when we had decided to move forward with Simon Says Give, I took an inventory of the people in our life and of the support we had from these people to bring our ideas to life. Once I identified the relationships we had in place, I could see the gaps of new relationships I'd need to build.

Reflect on your relationship with your siblings, your parents, your influencers in school and career. How have you built and maintained these relationships? What is out of sync and what can you do to nurture and lead the relationship to the next level? How have you let the O's you can't choose influence you and your decisions? Who are new O's with whom you want to create relationships to open new doors in your journey?

Reflect on how to build your relationship strategy. Who are your Inner Circle O's? Who else do you need in this Inner Circle? Who are your Catalyst O's? How much time are you spending with your Inner Circle and your Catalyst O's? Who is in your Close and Extended Community? How are you communicating to these others in your life?

THE FINAL STEP IN STOP IS P AS IN PLAN

The P in the STOP model stands for plan. The P is the culmination of the first three steps in STOP. The P step in the STOP model is the solid plan of action you need to make to move on toward your *Pinnacle Moment.*

Reflect on the O's you will need to help you build your plan. What are the obstacles you will have to overcome to put this plan in place? How do your talents play into the plan? Where do your O's come in to support you with the plan? Have you established specific and tangible goals in your plan?

The STOP model makes your *Unstoppable* journey simple. I have shared with you many instances throughout my life where I have put this STOP model to the test. The STOP model works both in personal and professional problem solving and works for individuals to organizational change. Don't be afraid to put yourself in front of others. Take risks or hire someone that has that as a talent. I have shared my *Pinnacle Moment*, which led me to

. . . .

We all have life challenges and losses. We all have a story to tell.

. . . .

the opportunity to be living out today. I look forward to hearing about your success in implementing the STOP model.

Recently someone asked me what I had done in life to think I had a book in me to write. I smiled at the question, because it really wasn't a question—it was a statement. I asked the person if they had ever been stopped in their tracks on something they wanted to do in life. Of course the answer was, "Yes." Then I shared that I wrote the book to share my stories of how I put the word *Unstoppable* to work in my life to help me break through in my personal and professional life. The "why" we are in business at Simon Says Lead is to help individuals and companies be *Unstoppable*. The book allows us to share the story.

My call to action for you is to look at your journey and be mindful of how it can impact your future as you look to simplify and solve the challenges in your personal and professional life. I took the time to share with you my life journey and examples of how the STOP model allowed me to be *Unstoppable* to inspire others to take the time to do the same. We all have life challenges and losses. We all have a story to tell. As individuals and as leaders, we are so busy with the pressures of a typical day, it is rare we take time to really reflect and evaluate. Take time to walk through your journey—you will be surprised at what you find!

We invite you to be in our Extended Community of others! We want you to share your stories with us on how you put the STOP model to the test. We welcome you into our Inner Circle to find ways to collaborate and be *Unstoppable* together. The second book in the *Make Unstoppable Simple* book series could be written in collaboration with your stories! We look forward to hearing from you.

BE *UNSTOPPABLE*.

Share your *Unstoppable* stories by visiting
Simonsayslead.com/unstoppable

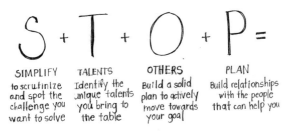

SIMPLIFY
to scrutinize
and spot the
challenge you
want to solve

TALENTS
Identify the
unique talents
you bring to
the table

OTHERS
Build a solid
plan to actively
move towards
your goal

PLAN
Build relationships
with the people
that can help you

REFERENCES

Covey, S. R. (2013). *The Seven Habits of Highly Effective People*
(Vol. Anniversary Edition). New York, New York: Simon & Schuster.

Fogarty, N. (2013). *8 tips for relationship building in business*. From Virgin
.com: http://www.virgin.com/entrepreneur/8-tips-relationship-building-
business

Neitlich, A. (2005). *How a Core Relationship Strategy Can Help You Increase
Profits*. Retrieved 2015 30-1 from Sitepoint: http://www.sitepoint.com/
core-relationship-strategy/

Schwartz, J. (2012). *B2B Services Marketing*. From Research Based Insight
From ITSMA: http://www.b2bservicesmarketing.com/category/strategy/

ABOUT THE AUTHOR

Dina Simon serves as the president of Simon Says Give®, and the chief executive officer of Simon Says Lead®. For more than twenty years, Dina has worked with Fortune 100 companies developing their greatest asset - their people. From talent recruitment to leadership development she has been recognized as a C-suite leader, that has built *Unstoppable* relationships with her internal and external clients.

In her role at Simon Says Give, Dina put on her corporate hat and know-how to work creating a start-up nonprofit to support her daughter Mandi's vision and mission to help kids in need. Their rapid success has gained national attention.

Simon Says Lead was established as a benefit corporation with proceeds benefiting the nonprofit. Clients engaged with Simon Says Lead and proceeds from this book have a direct impact on the nonprofit. Simon Says Lead works with individuals and organizations that want to break through and be *Unstoppable* in solving their challenges.

Dina and her daughter Mandi, speak on a national basis to share their experiences and entrepreneurial inspiration.

The Simon Family and the entities growing from the last name Simon, currently reside in St. Paul, Minnesota.

For more information about Simon Says Give,
visit simonsaysgive.org.

For more information about Simon Says Lead
and the services offered, visit simonsayslead.com.

Contact Dina directly, at:
dina.simon@simonsayslead.com or (612) 470-STOP